LS AOL ✓ **W9-ABB-356**

LETTERS FROM PAKISTAN

One Woman's Odyssey

Agnes Olive

ISBN-10: 1501045032
ISBN-13: 978-1501045035

Agnes and Dave Olive left their serene village of Terra Cotta, Ontario, Canada to live and work for three years in Lahore, Pakistan. The year was 1984. Dave was contracted to set up curriculum development for the polytechnic colleges. Agnes was invited to be artist-in-residence at the National College of Art. Dave's company had offered a bonus of around-the-world tickets for six months while bids for the equipment came in. The two lovers of travel could not turn down this offer.

Letters from Pakistan is a compilation of original letters by the author sent to family and friends.

FOREWORD

My dear family and friends

I am writing to again thank you for saving all my letters from Pakistan. This was indeed an act of love and encouragement.

I am following your suggestions to incorporate them into book form so we can all share the memories, and so my grandchildren may have some idea of the experiences and adventures that existed in their gene pool when they entered the great experience of life. I truly hope it will encourage them to adventure forth.

I passionately believe, that in order to live with peace and harmony on this universe, we have to honour and support the belief systems of other cultures, even and especially when they differ so widely from ours, instead of attempting by often violent means to try and convert them to our ways of believing. This is the legacy I hope to leave my children and their children; an insight into life in a totally different culture as experienced by their parents and grandparents. It was a great learning experience and helped me to realize how important humour is in our daily lives. We are often too serious.

If I had not had the deep friendship and support of Mrs. Masood and other Pakistani friends, I would never have had the opportunity to understand that they are just ordinary human beings with all the strengths and frailties that exist within us all. They were born into the Muslim faith as I was born Catholic and we are all on a path of learning.

I fortunately had the opportunity to reinforce this knowledge when upon returning from Pakistan, I taught ESL to adults. At times I taught as many as 16 different nationalities in one classroom. They all shared the same dream of living in freedom in Canada, and I felt very privileged to give them a small glimpse of our culture with love and empathy for their new experiences in a foreign country. My Pakistan experience definitely opened my heart and my understanding and I am so grateful.

Since the terrible events of September 11, 2002, news of Pakistan has come into our daily lives. I am now exchanging letters with Mrs. Masood. I tell her that we are concerned for their welfare and join her in praying that peace soon comes to that part of the world.

I pray that the women of the world will regain their collective voice and that the world will listen closely to what they have to say.

Instead of interference, let us give each other understanding and compassion, and may we all live in peace.

Namaste
Agnes Olive

1984 LETTERS

September 26, 1984
50-G Gulberg 111
LAHORE, PAKISTAN
Phone 872711 (when it works)

Hi dear friends and family:
This is my first letter home. It is also the first time I have tried to use the word processor and the first time I have tried to give my impression of Pakistan. I don't know which is the harder task. I think I would have to say it is trying to give a capsule view of Pakistan.

So much has happened since I arrived and it is certainly a country of many contrasts. I have had the most hair-raising ride of my life and walked on many beautiful, breathtaking trails through the foothills of the Himalayas. I guess the best way for me to handle this mammoth task is to start at the beginning.

I landed in Rawalpindi after a 24-hour flight from Toronto with stopovers in London and Dubai. It was great to see Dave and we stayed overnight at the Holiday Inn. He has been sick and lost quite a bit of weight but is fine now and thoroughly enjoying Pakistan in spite of the many run arounds he has been given.
The next morning we took off in our new Nissan with a

driver hired for the week. Before he turned on the key, I noted that he said a prayer. After we were on the road for a few minutes I knew why. This was the ride I referred to earlier, the most hair raising, spectacular, terrifying four hour drive of my life. It curved at what seemed to be a continuous 90-degree angle (impossible I know) and at every curve he had to sound the horn. The road was very, very narrow and had absolutely no guardrails. We passed one car that had fallen over the side and was on its roof on the road many meters below. When we met another car or animal or worse still killer bus (found out later that is what they are called) it was a game of chicken – who was going to budge first. I picked up where the driver left off and prayed the rest of the way.

Halfway to our destination of Nathia Gali, we stopped at a place called Murree and had lunch. I couldn't eat, but enjoyed sitting in the only, very basic restaurant and watching a parade of a most diverse group of people. I am very intrigued here with the clothing and have decided I like the men's much more than the women's. They wear a shalwar kameez, a long shirt slit at the sides over a pair of gathered pants, actually much like the women's only in plainer colours. They wear all sorts of different hats indicating which area they come from. As I sat there observing, I felt as though the movie "Caravans" was being filmed. Also, much to my amazement, the only clock hanging on the wall over my head started playing "home on the range." Today, only 12 days later, this would not amaze me at all.

Nathia Gali is a tiny hamlet at the foot of the Himalayas visited mostly by trekkers. We were the only people staying in a small group of cabins called Blue Pines, not great by North American standards but for Pakistan, it was cozy, (not a term to be used here very often) and we loved the three days. We decided, much to the amusement of a crew of old men, who turned out to be the staff, to have our meals served in the cabin. Dave had brought the two silver wine goblets given to us for our silver anniversary, a small portable recorder radio, some tapes and a bottle of wine, which he had managed to buy with his new government ration book. There were some candles in the room in case of power failure, but we decided to light these. We then had five courses of the most inedible food served to us by all five of the old men, each serving a different course. We had a fire roaring in the fireplace and I kept thinking, "this is quite civilized." Each day we trekked between 5 and 10 miles. The air was so fresh and energizing. When we packed up to leave, the five men competed with each other to carry out our cases. They finally settled it by three of them each carrying one and two sharing one small case. When we arrived at the car, they were all standing in a semi circle around the car waiting for yet more tips. The motel owner then came over, accompanied by another very, very old man, who said he had been guarding our car and it was customary to receive a tip for this service. Now, we were the only guests in the entire village, the only car in the parking lot, and we had a driver who was watching it. However, we gave him a tip and left having handed out almost as much in tips as in accommodation and meals. We did not have one edible meal the entire stay, unless you happen to enjoy stringy chicken for most meals and cold eggs for breakfast. I am used to carrying instant coffee, so at least the day started with a decent cup of coffee (comparatively speaking). I asked if we could have beef for a change, so the cook was sent into the village and promptly came back with the news that there was no beef available. Later in the day as I wandered through the local market, I came upon the meat section. Huge sections of meat covered in flies hung by the roadside. I silently thanked the cook.

We asked Qamar, our driver, to drive on to the next village and Dave and I met him there. We took a four-mile trek along the original old oxen trail cut out of the side of the mountain. It is a walk I will always remember. The sun was shining, there was a gentle breeze and the atmosphere was so clear we could see over to the mountains of Kashmir. There was absolute silence except for the sound of the wind and eventually the sound of a colony(?) of monkeys. We had never seen so many monkeys in their natural habitat and it was fascinating to watch them. We were told later that had we been eating, we would have been attacked. We kept thinking how we would like to share this trek with all our hiking friends at home in Canada. On one of our treks, we came upon some mud dwellings built into the side of the mountain. Thanks to Qamar, whom we met up with, and who speaks many dialects, we were invited inside. It was immaculate. The mud floors seemed to shine. There were two rooms, the first with a small table and metal stove and the second lined with beds,and, hanging from the supporting beams, rows of beautiful tinfoil cutouts. We were surprised to discover that not only did they have electricity but had acquired a big, shiny ghetto blaster. The elderly lady beamed with pride as she explained her brother had brought it back when he visited England. It seemed so out of place in the setting. We reluctantly left, especially me thinking about the drive home.

Speaking of home, we arrived at our new home in Lahore, a flat over the top of a house, very spacious, but barren. Gary, who shared the flat until my arrival, had arranged a welcome dinner for me. It was the first and last dinner cooked for me by Tony, who was about to be sacked the very next day. I guess this is as good a time as any to relate the current "Servant Saga." When Dave and Gary moved into the flat, they hired a cook named Joseph. Many of the working class have become Christians and have taken Christian names and hope they will be hired by the expatriate community. Joseph, unfortunately, was absent more than present and finally he did not show up for three days in a row. Dave decided to investigate and discovered that Joseph was in jail. Apparently, this is not an uncommon event. One couple told us they sent their cook out one day to buy a chicken. He pocketed the money and ended up in jail for stealing a chicken. To get back to Joseph, he did not want to permanently lose his job while in jail, so one morning his nephew Tony arrived on the doorstep complete with marvelous references.

Unfortunately, he followed in Joseph's footsteps and often did not show up. One day after a couple of days of "no shows," Tony reappeared and said he had not been able to come to work because the rains had washed his house away. Dave by then had heard every excuse imaginable, but went with Tony to his house. Tony lived in an area that housed many of the servants and Dave found the conditions deplorable. The next day the roof finally caved in on Tony's house, and Dave told Tony that he and his wife and child could live in the servants' quarters at the back of our flat. It consisted of one small cement room with an outdoor toilet and shower. That day Tony arrived with two kids and a very pregnant wife. She was to be our new cleaning lady. Well, not only could she not clean, but Tony was unreliable, filthy and dishonest. This was the domestic scene that greeted me on my first glimpse of my home. Gary related many instances and warnings he had given Tony and strongly suggested we get someone else.

Thus exited Tony and within twenty minutes entered George. "You need a cook memsahib?" My life in Lahore was about to begin. I couldn't believe it. How did word get out so fast? This was my first day here and I knew nothing about the routine of hiring servants. This was to be my new job, so I said "Come on in," and I am glad I did. George has been with us for a week now and so far so good. He has actually appeared every day. This may be in part because our landlady, Mrs. Masood, who lives downstairs, decided I needed some help in the hiring area, (an understatement) and had a long stern conversation with George that made me cringe. It was done in very polite terms, but the bottom line was that if George let us down in any way, he would have to answer to her because we were guests in their country and should be treated as such. We are paying him a bit above the current scale, 1200 rupees a month or roughly $120.

I asked him to be in charge of a cleaning person. The next day this quite attractive Moslem woman arrived in a flowing pink chiffon shalwar kameez. She was accompanied, of course, by her husband. I wasn't sure what George was up to but it didn't look much like this new gal was going to clean. I had to leave to go to a computer course to see how to use this machine. The next day, she didn't appear, so George the same day found another woman to take her place. Again I had to go off to my computer course and when I returned home found out that again the cleaner had not turned up. Out went George on another search and this time came back with Grace, who has been with us for five days. I don't know if this has anything to do with the fact that I have been around. Grace informed me yesterday that "Is hard work but God helps me."

So at the moment, all is well at the Olive household, but I have a feeling that I still have a lot to learn. There lingers a bit of a caste system here, even though they don't admit it. Grace cannot sweep outside. That is beneath her. George does not do the laundry. That is beneath him. Hence we now have a Dobi, a man who comes in once a week and does our laundry (except my underwear) in a big tub. The staff is expanding and I am starting to feel a bit like a prisoner in my own house. I cannot run around with my skin showing and it is hot.

I will now tell you something about our flat. It came furnished, is very roomy and has many more closets and cupboards than we have at home in Terra Cotta. It has a large living room with a gas fireplace for cool winter nights and is attached to a dining area. The kitchen has a gas stove with flames that leap to the ceiling when it decides to light. To get to the kitchen from the dining room, you have two choices. You can go through the living room and front hall or go outside onto the back patio and in through another door. I gave my first dinner last night. I say "I," as opposed to "We," because this is also part of my job description. It was also a farewell for Gary. It was so great to tell George what I wanted for dinner. I then slipped on a gracious afternoon frock and went out to the garden to select flowers for the table. Actually I did feel like I was in a Lady of the Manor Play as I snipped flowers from Mrs. Masood's garden and slipped them into a basket.

To get back to the description of our flat, it has everything but soul (and you all know how much I need soul). Since we arrived, I have moved the furniture around so much that Dave is getting dizzy. Now I have to get to work on an area rug to cover the cold terrazzo floors and hang something on the high, bare walls. I feel as though I am living in a gallery between shows. I have spent a bit of time looking at the local art and fear the walls may stay bare for a long while. We have a nice outdoor sitting area overlooking Mrs. Masood's garden and tomorrow I am going with Qamar to get some large potted plants. I cannot go out by myself, so thank God (or should I say Allah) for Qamar. We have three large bedrooms, each with its own large bathroom. Dave uses one room for his office, and that is where I spend some time each day doing some typing for the project and learning how to use this computer (another part of my job description). The office and our bedroom are air conditioned, but the rest of the flat has only fans.

The Pakistani people we have met so far are gracious and treat us as very special guests in their country. The first night just after dinner, a couple, Max and Mabrite, came to visit and say welcome to Pakistan. Max is Pakistani and Mabrite is Swedish.

They are married, and have lived as is the custom, in the home of Max's parents for six months. On the way to our house, they stopped and bought from a street vendor, three garlands of small fresh roses. On arrival they tied them around my wrists and said, "Welcome." A beautiful gesture. Two nights later we went out to dinner to a Chinese restaurant and invited Mabrite to go along. Max was away, and she said she would like to come as long as we understood that we would both have to come to pick her up and come in to meet Max's parents. Otherwise the outing would seem improper. We did this and were offered the usual warm 7 -Up. Everyone here lives on soft drinks or chai, a tea made with milk and many spices. After a brief conversation with mother, who spoke no English, and father, who spoke a little, we were deemed safe and proper enough to accompany Mabrite. Just before we left, Max's mother handed me a brown parcel and said, "welcome," in Urdu. In the bag was a complete Pakistan outfit for me; my first shalwar kameez. I was surprised and deeply touched. Mabrite offered me her bedroom, so I put it on and wore it that evening.

A few days later I received my first armful of Pakistan bangles. Mrs. Masood is a very liberal thinking lady and very well read. She has offered to be my mentor and whisked me off to the famous Anarkolis Bazaar, a huge bazaar that covers blocks and sells just about everything that is available in Pakistan. She said "Mrs. Olive, (she calls me that) you must have bangles. You cannot be in Pakistan without wearing bangles." I then found her slipping 36 bright shiny plastic bangles onto my arm. I don't think I will ever get them off.

I still haven't figured out the woman's role here, because I haven't been here long enough. In Nathia Gali, women's role seemed very straightforward. They went into the hills at 5 a.m., cut wood, or found small branches, piled it on their heads and walked approximately five miles back to their homes each day. The country gets 10 to 12 inches of snow, and the women reminded me of little squirrels getting ready for the winter. Until I left Nathia Gali I had not seen a woman without a load of wood on her head. Next Tuesday we are going to our first Asian Study Group. The subject is Women and the Koran. I read in the Muslim newspaper that Pakistani females constitute approximately fifty percent of Pakistan's population, but the labour force includes only three per cent of working and professional women. Total literacy rate in the country is only 27 percent, but in the case of women it is only 16 percent.

I am copying an article from the Muslim newspaper on Women and Economic Life which I thought you might find interesting. And so, you ask, what am I doing about my clay work? As you know I was supposed to be Artist in Residence at the National College of Art in the Ceramic Department. Well, I spent a couple of days there visiting with the instructor, who is tired and out of date, but not about to leave. The Ceramic Department is like Saturday morning at the "Y" and I just cannot see myself working there. There are three bored students and approximately 30 standup kick wheels all gathering dust. The kilns are very old and probably dangerous to use. I spent a day talking with the teacher who seemed desperate just to talk about his work. When I asked him if he exhibited his work he answered "who for?" I do not know what I am going to do, because there is no place for me to work in clay at the

Women and economic life

INAUGURATING the two-day seminar on 'Working conditions and welfare facilities for working women at Karachi on Nov. 27, the Sind Education Minister said there was dire need to take appropriate welfare measures for working women keeping in view the socio-economic milieu of the country. He also underlined that males and females were inalienable components of society and pointed out that Islam made no discrimination between the two where working for welfare and uplift was concerned. He illustrated his point by referring to Hazrat Bibi Khadija, one of the pious consorts of the Holy Prophet (PBUH), who was a reputed trader of her time. The Minister also threw light on obstacles confronting womenfolk in participating in economic life such as tradition, social inhibition, illiteracy and prejudices.

The present seminar is yet another welcome step towards bringing out women from the cloister of the household into the employment market so that they can contribute their full share towards the socio-economic uplift of the country. There is an imperative need for chauvinistic male-dominated society to accept women as equals in all fields of economic endeavour on the basis of merit and qualifications. There is no point in educating women and then confining them to the four walls of a home to engage in or conduct household chores. If rural women can share productive work with the menfolk, there is no reason why their urban sisters should be denied this opportunity. It is high time all prejudices against women were discarded. All efforts should be made to promote female education and qualifications thus attained should be put to productive use. For this, however, it is of the utmost importance that decisions taken at seminars such as the one under reference be implemented forthwith, unless all these exercises are to be reduced to so much rhetoric.

flat . Apparently there is another potter here who recently held an exhibition in a bookstore. I will get in touch with her soon. I do miss my studio and gallery. We will be leaving in December for a six-month hiatus with an around the world ticket, so will make up my mind when I come back. We are looking forward to daughter Caron being with us for Christmas and the trip.

I still haven't been to the old walled city, but the rest of Lahore is a mixture of some nice, tree-lined streets, and some filthy lanes with oxen grazing at the side or at times in the middle. Loaded donkeys pull carts full of furniture etc., camels proudly carry their loads of many wares. There are brightly painted killer buses and just ordinary rickshaws and cars, cars, cars. All are competing for the right of way. There is the occasional traffic light, which is basically ignored. Dave decided he had to learn to drive in these conditions in case we wanted the car when the driver is off. They supposedly drive on the left and fortunately Dave still remembers driving in Australia. After two ventures forth he is still alive. Thank God the Pakistani people don't drink.

So what do we do for social life. Just after I arrived, Dave took me to one of the big hotels for a special dinner. The meat here is buffalo and the better cuts are delicious. (either that or I am forgetting what delicious is). I am not a big meat eater, but we ordered the chateaubriand for two. I guess I wasn't ready for the fact you can not order wine, even in the large hotels. You have not lived until you have eaten chateaubriand with warm 7-UP.

Drinking alcohol is strictly forbidden in Pakistan and we can be turned out if we are found offering a Muslim an alcoholic drink in our homes. Certain positions here allow the expatriates to own a very precious C.B.R. book, which entitles us to a prescribed amount of alcohol in one year. We have to buy by the case and go to Islamabad to pick it up. We have more alcohol in our flat that we ever thought of having in Canada.

Isn't it so ironic. We share it with friends who do not have the book. I must admit that dinner with a glass of wine sure beats 7-Up. The other day in a little offbeat shop, we were amazed to find a couple of cases sitting in a pile of dust in a corner. The new owners didn't realize it was alcohol and of course it is against the law for them to sell it. We very casually bought one dusty case of Bristol cream sherry for 50 rupees (approx $5.00). We passed on the word to a fellow expatriate who sped off to the store and then slowly sauntered in and purchased the other.

Speaking of alcohol, I am enclosing a copy of a note we got one night from a man who came to our door to ask for brandy. Word gets out fast when an expatriate moves to town and we are considered an easy touch. This man pleaded for a small amount of brandy for his sick friend. Brandy is actually prescribed by the doctors here when they feel it will help. After much soul searching we gave him a very small amount for his sick friend. An hour later he returned with this note that we found to be hilarious. We refused this second request.

To continue on about our social life, (appropriately spelled in small letters), the other night we went to the American Club. As expatriates, we can join as social members, which means we get to use everything but the small swimming pool. They have a dining room, that serves lunch or dinner with cold beer, wine etc. It is very popular, and I can't believe it, but, already, I am dying for some wieners and beans! You cannot buy bacon here but it is served at the club. Some of the Americans have a special store where they can buy these imported things. We will definitely have to befriend a few. The Club, besides having a dining room, has a dart room with a dart club every Wednesday night and uncensored movies Friday and Saturday nights, plus a small bar and a small lounge. Believe me, after a while it appears to be an oasis in a desert. We are going over tonight. It is welcome back to old members after the summer and welcome to new. There is only one other Canadian couple here working for Bombardier, so I am glad we are welcome at the Club.

And now, another story concerning food. Jim and Sue, a couple with the Salvation Army are here running an orphanage and are more involved with the local people than are most expats. As a result, they have much information and many stories to tell. They told about having to throw out 40 boxes of cake mixes because they had been sent by sea and were stale and full of bugs by the time the lost shipment was found. (Someone had very wrongly told them that they could not get cakes in Pakistan.) Anyway, they sadly threw the boxes into the garbage and the next day saw them on the store shelf at a very high price. Their cook had retrieved and sold them. Needless to say, they were taken off the shelves.

We have looked into joining the Punjab club. It is very old English with formal sofas and hunt scenes on the wall. Very stuffy, but has a nice pool and tennis court. I don't think we will join. It isn't "US." We had hoped to take up tennis, but it has been too hot. It is starting to cool off now and the evenings are quite pleasant for a walk. To tell the truth, I haven't had the energy to play anything that requires much physical strength. The heat seems to sap my energy. Each day we meet new people and have new experiences. I guess when all this grows stale, I will look for further activity.

Another form of entertainment is visiting with all the salesmen who arrive at our door nightly, their bikes laden down with bags of brass, wood , rugs, etc. These wares are from Pakistan, Iran, Kashmir and Baluchistan, and haggling with the merchants is more fun than watching the terrible TV programs. Because so few have phones, (we are lucky to have one because we need it for the office), we also never know who is going to drop by for a visit.

One last story and then it is time to close. I wrote down all the details when I got home from buying our toaster because the experience was so unbelievable. Trust me, it has not been exaggerated.

This little story starts with a quiz "HOW LONG DOES IT TAKE TO BUY A TOASTER IN PAKISTAN?" The answer is two and one half hours, seven rubber stamps and a mini riot later.

Dave and I left home at 2:45 one afternoon with the simple task of buying a toaster. We headed off to the Duty Free store clutching our precious A1 form that allowed us to shop there for foreign goods. The place was already filled with foreign nationals, though we were the only white faces in the crowd. The store, we had been told, closed at 4 p.m., and Dave kept saying "We had better get a move on." I said, "Come on Dave, how long can it take to buy a toaster?" They will be the final words on my tombstone. Dave, now a three -month veteran gave me a "you will see" look.

To start the venture, we had to show our passports to get into the shop. We then went to the showroom and looked at three toasters all locked behind glass doors. We asked to see one out of the case. The salesgirl said this was against the rule, but she would make an exception and open the case for us. We carefully selected one and she made out a bill writing big XXXX's along the bottom to indicate it was our only purchase and pointed us downstairs. There, we joined a throng of Pakistanis all trying to receive their purchases. First, we went to a counter, lined up, and eventually had our paper taken by Official #1. He studied it very seriously and asked to see our passports. I felt as though we were buying the toaster for the K.B.G. He finally wrote something on the paper, stamped it and passed it to Official #2, who was standing beside him at the same counter. He stamped it and signed on the back and then passed it to another Official #3, also behind the same counter. Official # 4 repeated this act. We had now run out of Officials at this counter, so I thought "Good, now we will get our toaster," but such was not the case. Next we had to take our very stamped piece of paper to a wicket and pay for it. The store would not accept rupees, so we had to use our American Express. We then took this same form to another counter where it was copied by #5 and handed to another Official #6 who stamped the original and the copy and signed something on the rather crowded back. We were then sent with both copies into a very small, hot crowded room to have it again stamped and signed. This Official #7 seemed to perceive some problem, asked to see our passports and then called in Official #8. They had this very long debate all in Urdu and finally decided to rubber stamp the papers and again wrote something on the back. By this time, all the original writing and signatures were completely covered by rubber stamp marks.

Next we were sent to another wicket where we handed over our multi-stamped papers for a disc with the number 175 on it. This did not look good. We were then told to go down another flight of stairs to obtain THE TOASTER. We again entered a very hot, crowded room full of hot, frustrated people and our number was 175. It was by then of course after four o'clock. Along with the rest of the crowd, we were determined to get our purchases if it was the last thing we did – and it nearly was. After about another 20-minute, steaming-hot wait, the guards started to close the gates and told all of us we would have to come back the next day. What they did not count on was a crowd of irate Pakistani expatriates who had come God knows how far to make their duty free purchases. The consumers held onto the gate and wouldn't let the guards close it. The guards disappeared and came back brandishing Billy sticks, intending I guess, to beat us all into submission. The lives of many were saved by yet another official who gave the order to leave the gates open. At exactly 5:30 we clutched our toaster and bolted for the car, vowing this was our very last trip to Duty Free.

SEPTEMBER 29, 1984

I have decided to start a daily journal. I will start with yesterday, which was Friday, and the weekly holiday in Pakistan, sort of equal to our Sunday. I thought we were going to have a quiet day without George and Lady Grace, but it was not the case. I sauntered out to the kitchen in my nightgown, a freedom I cannot enjoy any other day. As I was battling the stove to come up with a pot of coffee, one of the servants from downstairs looked in the kitchen window to ask me a question and nearly had a fit because of my scanty attire. He wasn't sure whether to just cover his eyes or leap off the patio. I am finding it very difficult to have any privacy here because there are always so many people around and mostly men. I have started hiding up on the roof. I have a small mat up there and no one can come up on pain of death. Unfortunately, there is no shade so I cannot stay up there very long. Well, it turns out the servant wanted to bring the charpoys (rope beds used by the servants) from the third floor through our place and down into Mrs. Masood's and was told to ask us if he could also take the two that I had brought out of our servant's quarters and put on the patio. I needed something to sit on and was intending to have some big colourful pillows made. When I said "No, I want to use them, but thank you very much," Mrs. Masood appeared on the scene. It appears I have goofed once again. She told me in firm but kind words that it would not do for me to be seen sitting on the servant's charpoys. What would everybody including the servants think! She continued "Mrs. Olive I cannot sleep at night thinking of those ugly beds out on your porch." OK, OK, back they go. She loaned me one of her noirs (a bed made of woven cotton strips as opposed to rope and more suitable for her ladyship.) I immediately fell in love with the soft wide white strips woven around a wooden frame. With the downstairs servants help (they never seem to have a day off), I hung it on the wall to see how it would look (imagining it without the legs). It is the first thing I have seen that has creatively stirred me and I knew I had to have one or two hanging on our walls. I took it down before Mrs. Masood heard about it and put it back on the porch. There are absolutely no secrets here and I am sure the servant was already spreading the story downstairs of the upstairs memsahib putting a bed on the wall.

Later in the same afternoon, I decided to protein my extremely dry hair. I did not bring a big, all-covering housecoat which was a mistake, and came out of the shower wearing my bum length Japanese robe with a towel wrapped around my head. I walked into the living room and there stood Jay, another guy who once lived here for a few days before my arrival. He had come to pick up his clothes. He had arrived with his driver and cook and the cook insisted on washing the dishes in the kitchen. The doorbell rang and Jim and Sue stood there with a banana cream pie as an offering. A few minutes later Max and Mabrite arrived and we sat and chatted and ate the pie. I managed to throw on some clothes, but still kept the towel on my head. I dearly love people, but have got to find a place where I can hide when I need to. When I was a kid I always wanted to be the heroine of the comic strip "Scarlett O'Neil. She could press her wrist and just disappear.

SEPTEMBER 30, 1984

This morning Qamar and I took off for the market to find a white woven bed for the wall. As usual we caused quite a commotion as I strode along after my trusted guide. I soon realized I would have to have one made, and after much negotiation settled on 300 rupees with 150 down and I am to return tomorrow because I want to watch the man make the noir. He would weave an inner frame to be fitted into an outer frame with legs. This was perfect. I told him I had the outer frame at home and gave him the measurements. While trying to settle on a price, a Pakistani man came by and joined in the rather noisy negotiations. Of course we had drawn the usual crowd. He said "Pardon Memsahib, could I help." The guy who was making the bed was at this time insisting on coming to my house to measure the existing frame to make certain his would fit. I kept insisting, with Qamar's interpretation, (the conversation all took place in Urdu), that the measurements I had given him were fine. I did not want to tell him I was going to hang it on a wall nor, I think, did Qamar want to admit this. Finally, the stranger said, " Pardon but what is Memsahib going to do with the inner frame?" In frustration, Qamar finally admitted out loud that I was going to hang it on my living room wall. It was the first time I had heard SILENCE since I arrived in Pakistan.

Once the shock wore off, the stranger, Qamar, the maker and what sounded like the entire crowd all went at it again, but this time with much more vigor. I kept expecting a fistfight. (I should really talk to Dave about giving Qamar a raise.) After about five minutes of non-stop arguing, I was given the final figure and told to come back tomorrow at 5 p.m to watch the making.

That negotiation under my belt, I dragged poor Qamar off to the section where you buy the charpoys. I had already decided I was also going to have one of those on our wall.

These beds were just leaning up against the walls and we walked along the narrow dirt lanes trying to chose one. I love the rope beds as much as the noirs. The rope is woven in different patterns and they are truly works of art. It is so delightful to find beautiful design in every day objects. I finally decided on one with a painted blue metal frame and again the noisy bargaining began. I paid the 180 rupees and then told the old Baba that I wanted the legs cut off. He went into a sort of mini rage and refused to sell it to me. Qamar finally drew me aside and said, "Memsahib, we take and I cut for you." It is now hanging on one of the 11- foot high living room walls and looks great. The market was very hot and I was exhausted by the time we got home.

Thankfully George and Lady Grace had replaced the furniture in the living room. The terrazzo floors have been sanded and the place is starting to almost look livable. Next I have to discuss the possibility of covering the gold/red brocade sofa and chairs. That will be another day. Also time to start looking at carpets to partially cover the barren looking floors. We couldn't be in a better place for carpet shopping and want to take some home with us. That night, Dave and I put on some music, poured a drink and curled up in the living room with the intention of reading. The doorbell rang and one of the antique/brass dealers laden with wares stood there with an "I spent hours dragging these here to show you" look on his face. I told him I wasn't buying anything until I had a chance to get to know prices. Dave bought two brass/silver vases for 60 rupees each. And so ended another day in Lahore.

And now for a few "snippets" from our daily newspaper. I will include them throughout the book.

Two lovers caught dallying

FROM OUR
CORRESPONDENT

RENALA KHURD, Aug. 10: Roshi, young wife of Anwar (resident of Lundianwala) was arrested on Thursday by an Inspector of Police here along with her lover for flirting on a roadside.

According to the information supplied by the police, Roshi and one Mohammad Sarwar were found kissing and embracing each other just outside this centre. The Inspector who was on night Patrolling found the two lovers dallying on roadside under the cover of night darkness and apprehended them. Cases under the Hadood Ordinance have been preferred against the two lovers.

Man and woman caught misbehaving

FROM OUR
CORRESPONDENT

JAUHARABAD, Oct. 14: The police on Monday hauled up a man and a woman kissing each other shamelessly, exposed to public view on a roadside here.

According to the Police, Mohammad Akram, a resident of Hadali, a village near here, and Raza Khatoon of the nearby Bela village, casting aside all norms of propriety, were engaged in love-play. The police said afterward that the two lovers had apparently lost their aplomb, judging by the way they were wrapped up in each other on a public thoroughfare.

Two lovers held for having 'good time' in public

FROM OUR
CORRESPONDENT

KASUR, Oct. 2: The police have arrested Abdul Majid, a resident of border village Burj and Hanifan Bibi of a nearby village Maan, on the charge of "having good time" on roadside, exposed to public view.

According to the information available here, the accused were found, by some people passing by, in a compromising position, making obscene movements, near the border line. They reported the incident to the police, who arrived on the scene and apprehended the two philanderers.

The lovers have been incarcerated in the police lock-up, pending their trial.

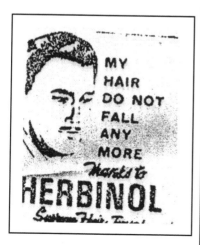

MY HAIR DO NOT FALL ANY MORE thanks to HERBINOL

OCTOBER 1, 1984

To day is Caron's birthday and I keep thinking about her and wish we were together. I am feeling very enclosed. I seem to need a mental and physical escape. Got up early and went out on the porch and read. I would love a breath of good fresh mountain air. When I felt this way in Terra Cotta, I could always walk out my door and go for a long country walk by myself. It is very hot and dusty here and it is also very improper for me to go out and walk by myself. I guess this is my first real test. I can't depend on Dave for company. He is always busy working. Yesterday, he did come with me to watch the noir-making event. It took exactly an hour and looks wonderful on the other living room wall. We also had an excellent going-away lamb dinner for Jay who heads back to Canada. Zella and Russ, a couple working for the same firm but living in Islamabad, came to the dinner along with Max and Mabrite. There is not much else to do here. Max showed his slides of Sweden and Norway.

Zella and Russ stayed over and today we went to the Shalimar Gardens. I was already feeling very down and the gardens did not help. There is such a strong sense of history here and of original beauty , but now the fountains don't work, the plants are well kept up, but the famous water pools are filthy and there is a general sense of decay and neglect.

My Ontario Potter's Magazine arrived in the mail today. So good to read it. There was a small write-up about Fireworks and also my raku show at the Burlington Gallery. My life as a raku potter seems so long ago. The weather is very humid and although it is getting cooler, I seem to have lost my energy. This depresses me because my mind still wants to do things, but the body is unwilling. I need to get away to the mountains for a couple of days and also to get outside of myself and start thinking of other things and other people. I need to do something creative. George is going to ask his neighbour to come over and show me how to weave a rope charpoy and I am going to have the wide cotton dyed and try and weave a noir.

Dave is quite excited about some multi presentation books Max loaned him. We have talked about some types of photo presentations we could do of Pakistan. I am particularly interested in modes of transportation. Yesterday I saw a mule pulling a cart with long construction metal retainers bent in a semi circle like a big horseshoe around the cart. I also saw a pair of oxen pulling a cement mixer and a guy on a bike carrying a bed on his head. I think these would make a marvelous photographic essay.

To day we priced joining the Terrace Club at the Hilton, which just means use of the swimming pool and sauna. The last thing I need is a sauna. They want $84 US a month for a couple.

Jay has decided to stay on longer and has moved in across the road. He has hired our original cook Joseph. Hope he stays out of jail.

OCTOBER 2, 1984

Dave & I went to our first Asian Study Group this evening. The speaker Dr. Riffat Hassan is a professor from Louisville University, Kentucky and has a doctorate in Theology. She spoke for 1-1/2 hours on women and the Koran. She is a woman in her 40's and said when she started ten years ago on her book on Women and the Koran, she was very angry and felt if she had not been born a Muslim woman she would not have had the difficult life she has had. She further felt that God whom she believes in, is a kind merciful entity and would not have meant women to suffer. She stated the problem was the interpretations of the Bible and the Koran by men. The original Koran was written in a special form of Arabic and many of the words and phrases could have multiple meanings depending on how it was interpreted.

She claims most of the problems of women and especially Muslim women stem from the interpretation of the story of Adam and Eve. According to her, there are four different interpretations of this story. One is that God made humanity not differentiating between man & woman and then of course the one we all know that first God made man and then woman to keep man happy. This automatically made her a secondary person. She also states that although the Muslims also follow this interpretation, strangely the story of Adam & Eve is not mentioned anywhere in the Koran. She was trying to understand why the Muslim women were supposed to have their bodies so covered up and did a study on early Greek philosophy. She found the concept that men were of the mind, but the women did not have much in the way of a developed brain and were of the body.

I am copying here a transcript from the Koran translated in 1974 by N.J. Dawood for Penquin.

FROM THE KORAN   Trans. N.J. Dawood,
Penguin 1974

WOMEN

Unequal:

"Men have authority over women because Allah has made the one superior to the others, and because they spend their wealth to maintain them. Good women are obedient. They guard their unseen parts because Allah has guarded them. As for those from whom you fear disobedience, admonish them and send them to beds apart and beat them. Then if they obey you, take no further action against them. Allah is high, supreme." (IV:34)

Modest dress:

"Enjoin believing women to turn their eyes away from temptation and to preserve their chastity; to cover their adornments (except such as are normally displayed); to draw their veils over their bosoms and not to reveal their finery except to their husbands, their fathers, their husbands' fathers, their sons, their step-sons, their brothers, their brothers' sons, their sisters' sons, their women-servants, and their slave-girls; male attendants lacking in natural vigour, and children who have no carnal knowledge of women. And let them not stamp their feet in walking so as to reveal their hidden trinkets." (XXIV:31)

Veils:

"Prophet, enjoin your wives, your daughters, and the wives of true believers to draw their veils close round them. That is more proper, so that they may be recognized and not molested." (XXXIII:59)

Equality of labour:

"Men as well as women shall be rewarded for their labours." (IV:32)

I guess we can conclude (my words now) that the women are kept covered so as not to provoke temptations of the flesh. The local newspaper is full of women being abducted or raped so I don't think this is the answer. Also the small village police are some of the worst offenders. Every morning I read snippets of information from various surrounding villages in the paper "Dawn"; e.g., two men went to visit a friend in his home and in the middle of the night abducted his wife; e.g., a woman was taken to a police station when she was found sitting in a theatre after the film was over. She reportedly could not find her friend with whom she intended to spend the night. Five police sexually attacked her and when she came before the judge the next morning, she was almost unconscious and her dress was all torn; e.g., a father drugged his daughter, wrapped her in a blanket and threw her off a bridge into a river because he did not want her to grow up in such a decadent society; e.g, a woman doused herself with kerosene and made herself into a human flame because her husband left her and their three kids.

And now for a few "snippets" concerning women.

'Pir', woman held under Hudood Ord.

BAHAWALNAGAR, Oct. 16: A fake Pir of MacLeodganj, 50 kilometers from here and a woman were held redhanded in a compromising position by people and handed over to police who arrested both and registered a case under Hudood Ordinance.

According to details, the so-called Pir, Zamir Hussain Shah, was carrying on the business of "Taveez and Gandas". On the day of the incident a woman Mst. Sakina wife of Noor Ahmed came to the Pir for a Taveez for a child. The Pir with his flattery persuaded her to fulfil his malafide intention and took her to his house.

His neighbour, Riaz Hussain came to know of his misdeed, and informed the people in the locality who caught the Pir and the woman while they were in a compromising position.

WOMAN BEATEN TO DEATH
Quarrel over cow-dung

By a Staff Reporter

A young woman was beaten to death in a quarrel over cow-dung near Badami Bagh on Wednesday.

The police have arrested two women, Inayat and Hajira, and two men, Shafi and Sharif, of the same locality in this connection.

It is stated that Aisha Begum, wife of Ghulam Ali, was collecting cow-dung near Buddha Ravi with her mother, Hussain Bibi. The latter had an argument with two other women, Inayat and Hajira, who were also collecting cow-dung nearby. As they started fighting, Aisha, who was at a little distance, ran to help her mother. Inayat and Hajira were also joined in the fight by their relatives, Shafi and Sharif. All of them started beating Aisha, as a result of which she died on the spot.

Aisha was the mother of a little girl and two sons.

Woman kills her abductor
From Our Correspondent

MUZAFFARGARH, May 12: A brave married woman shot her abductor dead with his gun saving her modesty at Chowk Sarwar Shaheed. Police have arrested the woman under Sections 307/302 PPC.

According to details one Allah Bakhsh of Chak No. 54/TDA abducted a married woman Musarat Bibi at gun point when her inlaws went for harvesting of wheat. The abductor took her to Chowk Sarwar Shaheed where he left her alone with his gun and went for making water. In the meantime Musarat availed the chance and shot at her abductor. He received serious bullet injury and succumbed to his injury at hospital.

OCTOBER 6, 1984

Today is a special day in Pakistan and is celebrated with what seems to me to be a very bizarre tradition. It is the 10th of Muhaarram, a time to honour and remember Imam Husain's sacrifice for Islam. To quote the Lahore newspaper, "Ashura the tenth of Muharramul Harrum, commemorating the supreme sacrifice of Hazrat Iman Hussain and his devotees in the way of Allah was observed throughout the country with utmost solemnity and religious spirit. On Saturday Oct. 6 Hussain along with his 72 companions laid down his life in the deserts of Karbala fourteen centuries ago while fighting against tyrannical rule. In the Islam religion, the word Shaheed, meaning martyr, has a halo of sanctity. Death is an immutable fact of life except for the martyrs whom God has kept alive. Martydom is the death of a person who in spite of being fully conscious of the risks involved, willingly faces them for the sake of a sacred cause" - end of quote.

According to my mentor Mrs. Masood, for three days Oct 8, 9, & 10th all the cinemas are closed and there is no music on T.V. I must admit I didn't even realize anything was different. Food is distributed to the poor and needy according to the paper. Mrs. Masood gave us a plate of spiced rice and on Saturday a plate of sweet rice. Both delicious. I don't think she considers us needy (except perhaps spiritually), but does try to help us relate to their customs. We both appreciate these gestures. We first heard about the "celebration" from an American. The Americans were warned by their Consulate not to go to the old city where the largest procession takes place in Lahore. They were told that there is an anti American feeling at this time and it could be dangerous. Mrs. Masood says that this is nonsense, but the danger is that the different Muslim groups sometimes get into a conflict and innocent bystanders could be hurt. I can believe this because it seems they are very prone to mob hysteria and it wouldn't take much to incite an incident.

The Muslim sects who celebrate Muharram are the Shias and the other sects are the Sunnis.

In spite of the warning, Dave & I decided to go to one of the processions. So off we went with a very nervous Qamar at the wheel. I think besides being our driver, he feels responsible for our safety and probably wishes we would forget these crazy notions. We arrived at one spot where the procession was passing, parked the car and got out. We were the only Caucasians and almost stole the show as a crowd gathered around us. We were in a small-enclosed area, and felt a bit uncomfortable. We looked up and saw some people on rooftops and asked Qamar to see if we could get on someone's roof. After much discussion, we were given a big bamboo ladder and with a few hundred eyes following us we climbed onto the rooftop. In the procession, groups of women were pounding their chests and you could hear the thumps keeping in time with their chants of "Imam Hussain". Also there were groups of men doing the same gathered in a circle around another man who was beating himself with a chain with many knives attached. The faster the crowd chanted, the faster he beat himself until his back was covered in blood. Young boys took part in this also. We saw many men walking around with their clothes soaked in blood. One of the central figures of this procession was a completely decorated horse representing the horse ridden by Hussain when he was slain.

We took many slides and also recorded the chanting in case we decide to give a slide presentation. It was extremely hot on the roof and one of the women sitting inside handed me an umbrella. A beautiful gesture. Once the procession had passed we headed back to the car and noted a first aid station wagon and also many pools of blood on the road. Later on the BBC we heard that a large riot had broken out in Karachi and the police had placed a curfew for a few days. Of course according to the local papers, there were no mishaps. George informed us that the people listen to a short wave program in Urdu for the real news. The newspaper is very controlled by the government in what it is allowed to print. I am glad we witnessed the spectacle, because otherwise, I don't know if I could have believed it.

OCTOBER 19, 1984

To day was a fun day, comparatively speaking. It is Friday and Dave & I decided to visit the old Fort. En route we saw a small crowd and a band. We asked Qamar what was going on. "It is just a wedding memsahib" answered Qamar with that "Oh no, here we go again" look on his face. Of course we said "Let's go have a look." This was a wedding of a very poor family. The house was an adobe structure and out in the front hung a colourful tarp and a sign saying, "Welcome". We edged our way into the crowd and as usual, every body stared because they couldn't figure out what we were doing there. A nice looking guy dressed in western dress came over and asked if this was the first Pakistani wedding we had witnessed. We said it was and would he enquire if the family would mind if we took some photos. The family said they were very pleased to have us as their guests and we were also very welcome to take some photos. We said thanks and that we would give them some of the photos. At this point the groom was being escorted down the dirt road to the brides house. He was lead by five uniformed men playing various strange instruments and every one was throwing one-rupee bills at the groom. His attendants would pick them up and make an apron by pinning them together. The groom wore this over the usual white shalwar kameez along with a tall pointed headdress made of strips of gold tinfoil. A couple of attendants were carrying a metal trunk on their heads. This contained gifts of clothing and jewellery for the bride from the groom's family. These gifts as well as the dowry the bride would offer had previously been arranged. The bride's gifts would be displayed at her house and everyone would view them when they came back from the church for lunch. Dave climbed up a hydro tower so he could get overview photos and I edged in as discreetly as I could to get the close ups.

This road we were standing in was a smelly open sewer and at times I thought I was going to be sick. The procession went into the canopied yard and we were invited in by the bride's mother and given a further invitation to come to the church and then back to the house for lunch. Before leaving we had a cup of tea and a small sweet. The tea was made in a huge brass pot and I just hoped it was boiled very well.

Qamar informed us that the huts were rent-free. I since found out they are considered squatters and one morning many months later, I sadly witnessed the complete community being bulldozed into the ground. To get back to the wedding, the tea and sweets consumed, we now squeezed a couple of extra little girls into our car and took off in a procession for the church. The groom's group on foot arrived before the bride's and we talked with one of the party who spoke a little English. He told us this was a Christian wedding in a Christian church, but was a traditional wedding in that the parents made the match and the bride and groom had never seen each other except from a photograph.

The bride finally arrived dressed in a long white dress and her face covered by a heavy veil. She seemed rather reluctant to go up the aisle and was held up and propelled forward by members of her family. She had two bridesmaids dressed in bright pink dresses. These were the first dresses I had seen worn since arriving in Pakistan. The church was an American Presbyterian Church on the property of a big college complex. It had been taken over from the Americans at the time of partition. The wedding was similar to a North American Christian wedding except that it was all in Urdu. The bride never took off her veil until they all went into a small vestibule, I guess to sign the register. When they came out and down the isle everybody threw confetti. The bride looked utterly sad and miserable. We were later told that the brides are usually sad because they are leaving their parent's home and will never live there again except for a traditional few days when she would go back to her former home. We did not go back to the bride's house, but promised to bring over some photos at a later time.

That same evening Max and Mabrite came over as pre arranged to introduce us to their Guru Mr. Engineer. That is really his name and he is also by profession an Engineer. He is a quiet, slim little man and talked to us nonstop in a very quiet voice for an hour whilst sitting on our couch in a full lotus position. The entire room seemed to be bathed in a feeling of serenity. (something very rare here) Max had met Mr. Engineer five years earlier when he was living alone and had become very ill. Out of nowhere Mr. Engineer appeared at his door and said "Come you need to see a doctor" He then took Max to a doctor who gave him some medicine. When Max offered to pay, he said don't worry, it is all taken care of. He has agreed to come over Monday night and discuss our getting into a meditation program. To my amazement, Dave seems to be interested. Probably because Mr. Engineer is also an Engineer. I have been meditating as you know for several years, and am very interested in having a deeper practice.

And now for a snippet regarding "marriage". A young girl is forced against her will into a 2nd marriage and attempts to escape.

Village girl being forced into 2nd marriage by her parents

BY A STAFF REPORTER

LAHORE, Aug. 22: Whereas. members of the fair sex in urban society have liberated themselves to a certain extent from the age-old spell of male chauvinism, women of the rural area continue to groan under the iron hold of masculine clan.

This is evident from a complaint received from a local engineer who happened to come across a soul-stirring episode in Chak No. 63/M of Tehsil Shujabad in District Multan, where an innocent married girl is being forced to marry another man in the circumstances, when she has neither been divorced by her husband, nor she is willing to seek the divorce.

The complaint indicates that in order to forestall her marriage which was being solemnised against her will, the poor girl tore up her bridal dress, removed the 'hena' from her hands and ran in frenzy after wrapping herself with a sheet of white cloth in the lanes of her village, crying at the top of her voice that she won't commit the sin of adultery, by marrying another person, when her husband was alive. She was, however, chased and caught and beaten up mercilessly by her father and other relatives. She was wounded badly. She is not being removed to nearby hospital lest she may escape from there.

It is stated that after her marriage, the relations of her parents were strained with her in-laws after a petty dispute over exchange of gifts. Consequently, the girl's parents hatched a scheme to humiliate her in-laws and decide to give her hand in marriage to another man without seeking a divorce from her husband. The girl who loved her husband resisted the attempt at the risk of her life. She is now on death-bed. Her desperate bid to unfetter herself from the shackles of false notions of prestige has so far proved a cry on the wilderness. it is anybody's guess, as to who will come to her rescue — organisations fighting for the rights of women, police or political parties?

NOVEMBER 12, 1984

Dave's boss, Ross, is arriving tomorrow so I am going to ask him to take this back and mail it from Canada. We are all in great shock and in mourning over the death of Mrs. Ghandi. The Pakistani people appear to want to keep a good relationship with India and are very concerned because India had earlier stated that Pakistan was helping the Sikhs in the whole Armritzar incident and of course it was a Sikh who was responsible for the assassination. The Pakistan Government called for a day of mourning and everything closed down for one day.

We thought of canceling our Christmas plans to go to Delhi, but things seem to have quieted down. The election there is on December 24 so we will wait until the 29th. Apparently one of the bigger hotels holds a big New Years Eve bash with music and dancing. I hope it is not too big a shock for our system all at once. Caron has arrived safe and sound and it is so great to have her here. The two of us spent most of Christmas Day in tears. Christmas has always been a very important day for our family and we missed Mike, Steve & Natalie and our dear friends. We are going to shop in Delhi and get ourselves a sari for New Year's Eve.

We picked up Caron in Rawalpindi and spent two days with friends in Islamabad to give her a chance to rest up and see a different area of Pakistan. The three of us ordered snakeskin shoes to be made and then headed to Lahore by car, a six-hour trip driving alongside caravans of camels, oxen, and donkeys. We were invited over to the home of the American Consulate for an evening of caroling and to trim the Christmas tree. Two nights ago we were invited to a mindi, a wedding party normally for the bride and women only.

This was unusual, in that a Pakistani family was giving it for non-Pakistani friends, who had been married in France three days earlier. It was the most marvelous evening of folk singing and dancing with everyone (men, also – a rarity) joining in. We were invited because it was given by a new acquaintance and hopefully a good friend when we return. She is a potter and one of the most unique people I have ever met. Her name is Scherezade and she has just returned from a one-year study in England.

Her husband is head of Painting at the College of Art where I was supposed to work. He has invited me to use the printing studio when we return from our Round the World Trip.

NOVEMBER 13, 1984

We went to our first dance last week at the American Club and it felt good to dance again. It was a mixture of Expats and Pakistani people, some of the more liberated ones do dance and drink. It is against the law for them to drink, so they do take a risk drinking in public.

Our Guru has left for a few months and Dave and I have become lax about our meditating. We seem to lack discipline. It is so easy to be lazy here. It seems the less we do, the less we want to do. I had my first Pakistani haircut yesterday. I was trembling when she started cutting, but it looks OK. It took 15 minutes and cost the equivalent of $3.50. I still seem to spend a lot of my time floating around, discovering markets. I work on the computer, a few hours a week for Dave and Jay. I had to negotiate a salary and said I would not work for less than the maid earned. We reached an agreement and it works out well because I can do the work in my own hours and it gives me some of my own money. I am used to having my own income from the Gallery and sales of my clay work and it is not easy to feel dependent again.

We are attempting to play tennis. It costs us $40 a month and for $2 more an hour we can play with a coach, but I'm afraid it is not my game. I may take up golf just to get out and do some walking. It is very difficult to walk here and I am getting flabby. I am not allowed to walk alone. Expatriate women have to be very careful of their image. They are considered whores until proven otherwise, thanks to the many x-rated videos on the market. The weather is in the 70s and today we are going swimming at the Intercon Hotel. We pay by the month, but unfortunately it closes for December. People think it is cool here and the old choqadoor (guard at the gate) is wrapped up in woolen shawls and hat.

NOVEMBER 15, 1984

This morning we had a private flute concert in our driveway. A snake charmer came by and was allowed inside the gate. Dave ran and grabbed his camera and we, along with three servants and the five servants from downstairs, came out to see his act. It was to be our first SNAKE CHARMER EVENT. The guy sat down and started playing his flute just like in the movies, and Dave had the camera ready for the big six foot cobra to appear. Finally after much playing, the guy reached into the basket and pulled out a tin from which he extracted a six-inch snake. I thought Dave was going to keel over from laughter. The servants also started to ridicule him in Urdu and he left saying he would be back on Friday with a bigger snake. You have to take entertainment here where and when you can get it.

On the domestic scene, Lady Grace, our cleaning lady, has left. Cleaning was beneath her, and she let us know it. She also gave the impression that we were beneath her and not even her talks with God could help her. Her replacement is Behira, and so begins a new drama.

I have been trying to buy a floor polisher and finally realized they just don't exist here. I mentioned this to Qamar who said "No problem memsahib, I find polisher." So off we went to the old market and again I am trailing along behind him, past stalls of old machines, etc. As usual we drew a lot of attention, because women just do not go to the machine market. Finally, we came to a store where they made furniture and there stood a boy polishing furniture. Qamar said "Memsahib, here polisher." That is why I am taking Urdu lessons.

Speaking of Qamar, the following is a note from him telling us that he has to go to his village because someone is dead there, and his son, who is delivering the note, brought the keys to the car.

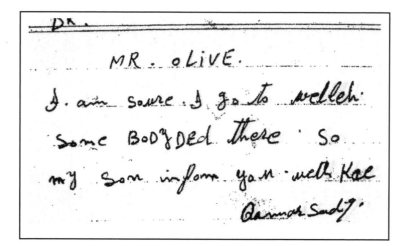

We have been to two weddings. I told you about the first one that we crashed. Well, the second one we were invited to and it was considered socially upscale from our first. When we arrived, I was told, much to my surprise, to go to a separate area that was just for women. I gave Dave a desperate look and followed my hostess. I was the only non-Pakistani there and not one of the women spoke English and my Urdu is limited. For two and one half long hours I sat and smiled. It turned out that the men were downstairs eating and when they were finished we were fed. Meanwhile, we sat in a row on chairs and the mother of the bride held up item by item, all the gifts the family of the groom had given the bride. All the clothing was sealed in plastic and looked very strange being held up for us to view. Again these gifts were part of the marriage contract. The groom was a doctor, but his parents still selected his bride and the couple had only seen photos of one another. The house of the bride was completely covered in a type of outdoor Christmas lights and at night you could see them for blocks. The night before, a band played in front of the house and the guests (including us) watched a guy wearing a black wig and white costume with bells and bangles on his legs, do the most amazing dance. He jumped all over the place with a long, eight foot pole on his head and on top of the pole perched a huge clay pot full of water. He balanced this contraption while we watched him dance for at least 20 minutes non-stop. The accompanying band members were all dressed in similar costumes and across their red shirts was printed COCA COLA. Apparently the father of the groom is the president of Pakistan Coca Cola.

NOVEMBER 17, 1984

Ross called this morning to ask if we could meet him and his wife Maryanne at the airport and could we arrange to have a dinner tomorrow at our house for them and three officials from the Asian World Bank. What could we say? Of course we said "Of course."

I was not too worried because I thought George could manage it with one day's notice. He had yesterday off and went to Peshawar to meet with his family. We had recently been informed that George has three wives, so weren't sure which family he was visiting. Peshawar is a fascinating ancient city near the Khyber Pass, about a six or seven hour car ride from here and a place where many of the Afghani refugees come to sell their carpets, pillow bags, etc. George said he knew where to buy some good ones at good prices. We gave him a fair bit of money to shop for us and I just hope we see him again. He is supposed to be back tomorrow morning to start work at 8.a.m.

At 8:30 the next morning, when George had not arrived, we sent Aslam, his brother-in-law and our latest cleaner to George's house. He informed us that George was not coming on the early bus, but would be here at 12 noon. I was still fairly calm about the dinner, and took off for the market to buy fresh salmon (no mean feat) and decided that George could whip up this wonderful salmon casserole that he makes and I would get Jay's cook Joseph (our former cook before he went to jail) to come over and give George a hand with the rest of the meal. I went across the road to Jay's and discovered that Joseph had sent a message that he was ill and would not be in. I said, "Never mind, Agnes, Aslam can help George, and I will get busy and set the table." At noon we sent Jay's driver Benjamin off to the bus depot to pick up the illusive George. Panic was now beginning to set in because I am a disaster in our kitchen. It is hard to believe I have been cooking all my life.

Dave finally said, "Look, we have to go and pick up Ross. I will explain the situation to him and we will go out to the only decent restaurant in town. We will invite them to our house tomorrow night. When George arrives later today, he can make some little snacks and we will serve them drinks before going out." Aslam took off on our communal bike to again check in with George's family and came back with the message in his best-broken English that George was not coming back. We didn't know if that meant for today or forever. Meanwhile we were committed to come up with a big company dinner for tomorrow night.

Dave then took off for the airport in our car, followed by Benjamin in Jay's car, because the Nissan is too small for Ross, Maryanne and their entire luggage. Meanwhile back at the airport. Benjamin had somehow managed to lock his keys in the car. Fortunately, another driver from the Asian Development Bank had arrived, so Ross and entourage were deposited at the Hilton and Qamar had to go back to the airport with a second set of keys to bail Benjamin out. It is now 20 minutes before they are to arrive for drinks and I am not going to serve any snacks. They may as well see what it is like here. Why should we try and make it look any different than it really is?

It is now two days later, very, very early in the morning. I will try and relay the events of yesterday before I forget (although I don't think I ever will). Dave had an early morning meeting and left very early before George was to be here to make breakfast. When Dave got home he said "I hope it is OK, I have included Mr. and Mrs. Toor in tonigh'ts dinner." What he didn't know is that just a few minutes earlier, Aslam had arrived to say that again George did not arrive home and he did not know when he was coming. There was no way we could cancel the dinner a second night, so I went across the road and asked if we could borrow Joseph to cook the dinner. Fortunately, he had decided he was well enough to come to work. I explained the situation to a rather hostile Joseph (after all, we had fired him earlier), and told him I had all this salmon sitting in the fridge waiting to be cooked however he wanted to do it. He informed me that he didn't do salmon. I realized that more disaster was imminent unless I let him select the dishes he knew how to cook. Of course this meant reshopping, which can take half a day, but off he went to the food market. I had decided the night before to meet Maryanne and with Qamar we would go to the market and buy her a shalwar kameez, because their entire luggage was lost at the airport. I sent Qamar to pick her up. Two hours went by and no Maryanne and no Qamar. I was beginning to feel as though I was in an extremely bad soap opera. I phoned the Hilton and paged Maryanne only to be told she wasn't there. Eventually she and Dave and Ross arrived. The plans had been changed. They both wanted to go shopping and see the market and then tour the old city. We spent a very hot but pleasant three hours shopping and touring and dropped them back at the Hilton to freshen up for dinner. Of course I kept wondering what was going on "back at the ranch."

When we got home, there was no one in the kitchen. Panic! I ran across the road and was informed by Joseph that he could not cook in our kitchen, but would cook it at Jay's and carry the whole meal across the road.

I set the table, had a shower and about 30 minutes before all the guests were to arrive, in strode George grinning from ear to ear and dressed to the nines in all new clothes which he had obviously bought with some of our pillow bag money. I was so angry with him, but Dave was delighted to see the beautiful pillow bags he had bought. I was in the middle of telling George how upset I was, and that I didn't believe that he couldn't get a bus for two days. They run practically every hour. While we were going through this drama, the doorbell rang and there stood a brass dealer with three of the largest copper pots I had ever seen. You could fit three people into one (and maybe at one time, they did just that). We told him we had guests arriving at any moment and did not have time to look at them. He informed us he had brought them all the way in a taxi, and asked if he could please leave them until tomorrow and then we could discuss the matter. The door bell again, and our guests waded their way through a mound of pillow bags, a chastised George, a brass dealer and three huge pots.

At that point I didn't even try and explain and told George to leave, that he was too late to be of help. Joseph and Aslam ran back and forth across the road with the food and it was delicious. We drank a lot of wine except for Mr. and Mrs. Toor who sat like wooden statues at the table. I didn't hear her first name when her husband introduced her, so I politely asked her what her name was. She said, "Mrs. Toor", and so went the evening.

To add the final touch to the evening, Joseph was late leaving after serving dinner and cleaning up and got picked up by the police on the way home and questioned until three in the morning. It seems that if Pakistanis are walking around late at night, the police want to know why. They do not bother them if they are driving a car or on a motorcycle. Of course Joseph had already had a sojourn in jail, so they kept him longer. I paid him generously for the evenings' work.

NOVEMBER 21, 1984

It is 5 a.m. and I thought a very good time to start my Christmas epistle. I hope you do not mind these group letters. It is one of many advantages of the computer. The reason I have selected this ungodly hour is that we are surrounded by four mosques with huge loudspeakers and one is pointed directly at our bedroom. Every morning at sunup, roughly 4.45 a.m., the speaker calls all Muslims to prayer. This goes on for about an hour and "The Call to Prayer" sounds like a million lost souls rising from their graves. In the summer the air conditioner drowns them out, but now weather in Lahore is very pleasantly in the 70s F, so we don't need the air conditioner.

I have been spending most of my days meeting new people, both Pakistani and expatriate, attempting to decorate the flat, learning to golf, learning to speak Urdu, learning about carpets (of which there are millions in Lahore) learning how NOT TO GO to my studio each day, learning how to hire, fire and exist with servants, learning where to find things in the many bazaars, learning about the culture of Pakistan, learning how to be waited on (not surprisingly, I adapted to this quickly) and learning to shower without water. If the downstairs gardener or the dobi turns on the water, the shower completely shuts off. This has proven to be most interesting, because the cultural norms do not allow me to just wrap a towel around my body and run out and ask them to shut off the water until I finish.

I told you earlier about my two beds on the wall. I managed to make a third noir on my own. I took the white cotton to a dye man who sits out in the dye market with marvelous big pots of dyes and keeps adding different colours of dye powders until you are happy with the test strips. I love this direct approach and my third bed is in varying shades of turquoise. Every time Mrs. Masood gets a chance she brings her guests up to see "Mrs. Olive's three beds on the wall." I have finally convinced her to let me cover her prized gold brocade sofa and chairs with a plain woven, off-white cotton. She cannot fathom that I want plain cotton over gold brocade, but doesn't argue any more. We bought an off white wool area rug (insane I know) for the living room and are enjoying the now stuffed Afghani pillow bags that the now forgiven George bought for us in Peshawar. I still miss a yard or garden to sit out and think of Terra Cotta and all those trees and grass and of course the swimming pool.

Dave and I have finished eight Urdu classes. The first two phrases I learned were actually from Qamar: "How much does it cost?" and then "Very, very expensive", to be stated with a look of horror and utter disbelief on your face. These two phrases pretty well get me through the market scene.

Learning about carpets is much more complex. Lahore is the rug city of Pakistan with many factories and many homes involved in cottage industry. There for a long time has been much dispute about young kids working in the factories with no opportunity for education other than the rug trade. The lighting is often very poor and they become semi- crippled from squatting in one position day after day, year after year. This, we are told, is now being changed, but not sure just how. We still saw young kids (mostly boys) working. Their small fingers are much more agile for weaving the finer carpets.

Dave and I spent a fascinating day in one factory. The owner very proudly showed us all the aspects of rug-making, from the designing to the dyeing in the big pots. Only small parts of the design are given each day, because otherwise, according to the owner, the weavers would steal the designs. Most of the designs we saw, derive from variations of Persian Carpets, with some colour and design changes. The general rule of thumb for pricing is to cut the original asking price in half and then start bargaining. Dave likes the new carpets and chose a beautiful turquoise 3ft. X 5ft. I prefer the old beat up ones the Afghanis carry around.

Re: learning about servants, what can I say? I cannot keep up with them and have to admire their originality when it comes to reasons why they can't come to work on any given day. As I write this I have just received a note delivered by Aslam written by George telling me George is too sick to come in. Aslam said that George is sick from all the polluted air. (I made the mistake one day of saying the air is so polluted that I can't understand why everyone is not sick). Of course, George, who is very swift, picked up on this. The truth of the matter is that his wife (which one?) has just returned from the USA and he wants to be with her. The other day a Pakistani man and proclaimed Christian came to our door to warn us about George. He told us in his most pious manner that 1. George is not a good Christian and should not be working for us because he sold his wife's services to expats. 2. He has three wives (I guess business is good) and 3. He stole a large amount of money from a Japanese family for whom he worked and therefore is blacklisted in Islamabad. 4. He was fired by a Danish family because he stole and sold their liquor. I do not find any of this difficult to believe, but at least now I may have a certain strength knowing some of his faults. I think I may just bring back a trusty new microwave, a washing machine and a floor polisher and fire everybody.

Of course I could not fire Qamar because he is my key to getting out. His latest game is using our car as a taxi while we are away. We trusted him with the keys because he had to pick us up at the airport. He probably would have gotten away with his "moonlighting" except that the guy who sold Dave the car recognized it and squealed on Qamar. He told us we should not let him continue to work for us, but Dave and I are so soft and besides he seems now like part of our family.

I believe I mentioned that Lady Grace floated out of our lives to be replaced by Behira who has since been replaced by

George's cousin Aslam. He seems to be a very nice young man, does not speak one word of English and is the only one who turns up regularly.

Here is a copy of George's note: - Roughly translated it says, "I am sorry today I am home with fever and cold. For that I not come on duty. I been to doctor this morning and I go tomorrow again.

DECEMBER 28, 1984

It is now December 28 and I am quickly trying to wrap this up so the computer, printer, etc. can be packed up. Our tickets are confirmed and we are leaving for Delhi tomorrow. As part of the contract, Dave's company has given us three round-the-world tickets for six months; they included Caron, who is still living at home. She is postponing her first year at university to travel with us. After Delhi we will spend time resting at Goa and then on to Sri Lanka, the Maldives, China, the Philippines, Japan, New Zealand, Fiji, and Hawaii.

Speaking of Caron, the two of us went out to the golf course recently to just get out on our own and do a bit of practice. Unfortunately my caddy, instructor, Shameer, did not show up. He is both my right and my left arm. He tells me where and how to hit, when to blow my nose, what iron to use, etc. He also usually provides the tees. I went over to the man in charge (don't know what he is called) and asked him to send Shameer out to meet us when and if he showed up, and could he please get us two tees. He smiled and disappeared. Caron and I waited for what seemed like hours when finally some guy came over and said "Memsahib would you like to sit at a table?" I turned around and saw a waiter approaching us carrying a large silver tray with two cups of tea. It pays to have a sense of humour.

Dave is enjoying the freedom and challenge of the job and performs his duties with "much fervor and enthusiasm," a phrase used here in the papers to describe how everything is handled. He spends most of his work time in the office with the odd trip to the Ministry and seems to enjoy the casualness of the setup. I miss my creative endeavors but in spite of the erratic electric load sheds when I lose all the work on the computer, I rather enjoy the word processor and both Dave and I have been amazed at how well we have worked together. I did have to threaten to go on strike in order to get the same Christmas bonus as the cook etc. We finally called Caron into arbitration and Dave coughed up the bonus.

We have loved getting letters from home and look forward to seeing you next June when we return for a short while to Canada. Our love and very best wishes for a Happy 1985 and may you never be such an unfortunate guest as poor Mohammad Akram whom you will read about below.

Sahib and Memsahib Olive

Guest drowned in village well

FROM OUR CORRESPONDENT

RENALA KHURD; Oct. 10: Mohammad Akram who was staying as a guest in the house of Mohammad Ali in Bama Bulla, a village in this area, was drowned on Tuesday in the host's well.

During his stay a bucket fell in the well. Akram immediately jumped in to the water pit to retrieve the pail but he was not able to get out. though he made three futile attempts.

As bad luck would have it, all the three times he tried to climb up, the rope snapped. At last, visibly, exhausted the ill-fated and somewhat guest called it a day and died in the well.

The police have registered the case and are investigating.

Mother Teresa in Lahore

Here we are in our newly renovated living room

Practicing darts

Appliquéd hanging from Rhajastan

Sheherezade and Agnes in Terra Cotta, Canada

Sugar cane factory near Peshawar, Pakistan

Agnes and Susan of the World Bank at a paper factory

Crazy Golf Day (charpoy on the wall)

Agnes on a camel safari in the Thar Desert, Jaisalmer, India

Agnes with a basket in Shangrila, Northern Pakistan

1985 LETTERS

January 18, 1985
50-G Gulberg 111
LAHORE, PAKISTAN
Phone 872711 (when it works)

Greetings from Goa Beach in India. Just imagine a long warm sandy beach adjoining a small Portuguese fishing village with the temperature in the low 80s. That's where we are and what a glorious change from the hot, dry, dusty city of Lahore.

Yesterday morning at sunrise, camera in hand, I walked along the beach for a couple of miles and the sound of the waves was so peaceful. On my way back, the small fishing boats were arriving with their catch of the day. I stood by and watched as the women and children sat in small colourful groups sorting the fish, shrimp, crab and an occasional lobster. This morning there was a huge tortoise in a net and they were all rejoicing. When all the sorting is finished, the catch is put into gorgeous big handmade baskets and the women carry them on their heads to be sold. We are living on seafood and local fruit - cheap, healthy and delicious. Each morning we sit on our little porch and wait for the fruit lady to come along, lower the basket off her head and then we chose our fruit for the day. What could be more direct? It costs us each approximately $5.00 a day including lodging and some young travellers are managing on $3.00 a day.

Colva is known as the nude hippy beach and the attire is any-where from none at all to topless. Then the occasional Sikh family comes along, and the women go in the water in their full dress. Dave, who has not seen much more than ankles in six months is in a constant state of rapturous shock. It is quite comical on Sundays. Buses bring people (mostly young Indian guys) to the beach. The outing is advertised as "Come and see the nude hippies." The guys, cameras in hand, and dressed in suits, ties, and shiny shoes, walk up and down the beach. What they try to do is stand behind a group of young nude girls, and a friend at a distance takes their pictures and they go back and pretend they are all together in a big party. If they are caught, they stand to lose not only their film but their cameras as well. I guess the risk adds some zip to an otherwise ordinary Sunday.

Goa is a small, predominantly Catholic town and belonged to Portugal until 1961 when India took it over. This morning we rented bikes and toured around the small outer Villages. We have been here now for a week and so far the three of us are traveling well together. I start each day with an early walk along the beach and then meet Dave and Caron at one of the many huts along the beach. I slide into a lawn chair at a little table, dig my feet into the cool sand and have a tall glass of warm milk with coffee and a banana pancake with fresh mango and honey syrup. The total cost is 35 cents.

To back up a bit, as planned, we spent New Years in Delhi. We left Lahore in a mad rush, and had to work Christmas day to get out on time. This added to our already depressing day, so we decided we deserved a couple of days at the Taj Mahal Hotel in Delhi. Our first evening and dinner there will stay engraved in my mind. We all ordered Italian food and it was served with wine on a candlelit table with a white tablecloth. Soft music played in the background and we danced. I thought I had died and gone straight to heaven. Until that evening I had not realized just how restricted I felt in Pakistan and how adaptable the human being can be. When Dave and I were newly married and lived in semi isolated northern Alberta, my landlady said, "Agnes, if you want to survive in this world, you will have to learn to be very adaptable." That sentence often comes to mind, and Pakistan has really put me to the test.

From Delhi we bussed to Rajasthan – a storybook land and hence my favourite. It is the land of the early Maharajahs with castles of pink and yellow perched on top of hills, very Dr. Seuss. In the Pink City of Jaipur, we had our first (but not last) ride on an elephant that took us up to the castle. We were anxious to get to the sea so decided to postpone our four-day camel safari near Jaisalmere until our next trip. It meant a 14 hour train ride. Instead we took the overnight train to Bombay, and from there to Goa. We paid our first baksheesh (bribe) to get the train compartment that we hadn't booked. It certainly beat the lineups and just shows how quickly we succumbed to corruption. But then getting seats on busses and trains truly tests our integrity. We have a bit of a system now for the buses. I grab a seat for the three of us while Dave gets on top of the bus and Caron hands up the luggage. Getting the seat is one thing, but holding it is quite another, as people are climbing in through the windows. I decided on my next trip through India, I am going to wear a nun's habit. The waters seem to part for them. Much to our surprise, we enjoyed Bombay more than Delhi. Perhaps because it is on the water, but also it is livelier. We also witnessed the lowest of existences here. On the main road to the dock area, we walked past shacks made of cardboard or whatever could be scavenged. People live in these and cook and wash on the streets and all day and night breathe in the fumes spewed out by the congested traffic. Little girls play on the street in immaculate white dresses that reminded me of the old Rinso soap ads. How do they keep so clean under these conditions? We have become hardened to the beggars. I think there is just so much poverty that we can't truly take it in.

The sun is about to set and we are sitting on the front porch in Goa thinking how we regret to leave tomorrow, We are going to spend approximately four more weeks heading south, partially by an inland water route and then onto the Maldives for some snorkeling and Sri Lanka for some Buddhist culture.

I am now skipping ahead five months and give you a very brief summary of the remainder of our trip. We have thousands of slides to show you. Sri Lanka was reeking with early Buddhist culture and a dead horse on the beach. The Maldives was as tranquil and perfect as we had hoped and hard to beat as a snorkeling haven. We from there landed in Hong Kong and actually used it as a base and stayed there three different times. It is a great place to shop and the YMCA is reasonable and in a first rate location, but you have to book it ahead. From there we took The Slow Boat to China. We traveled through China for about three weeks and it was an incredible experience. China is not set up for the individual travelers and it was extremely difficult trying to get a room or a seat on a train or plane or bus. I remember thinking, "If you can travel on your own through India and China, you can travel anywhere in the world." It was cold and gray the entire time and Dave finally got fed up and after two weeks headed for the Philippines where we caught up with him later. Caron and I then headed to the tombs in Sian. The clay soldiers and horses are without a doubt the most remarkable site I have ever seen. It was interesting just to have the two of us traveling alone. We found ourselves stranded in Sian with no way out for days (a long story). Luckily a tour bus arrived full of people from San Francisco. We gave our long sad story to the driver, who asked the passengers if they would mind if we headed back with them. They all said "Welcome Canadians" and Caron and I are grateful to them forever. When we finally returned to Hong Kong we spent a few days just to rest up and, yes, have a Big Mac in one of the best McDonald's in the world. I never eat them in Canada, but after the terrible food of China, that hamburger was King.

We flew into Manila in the Philippines, and stayed at a YMCA where Caron was introduced to her first huge cockroaches. We also met an interesting woman who in earlier years had been a Miss Philippines beauty queen. She had married and since divorced a German man and she now ran a bar in the red light district of Irmeena in Manilla. She explained to us that gold jewellery is used as security in pawn shops in the Philippines and that is how she bought her bar. She offered us room in her car as she too was heading for the Island of Boracay. This is an island, an absolute paradise of white sand, and old outrigger sail boats. We met up with Dave there.

Then, back to Hong Kong and onto Japan, one of my favourite countries. I love the aesthetics, the gardens, the theatre and ordering food by pointing to exact replicas made of plastic. I was surprised how few people spoke English. They do have an interesting custom: you can visit a Japanese family in their home for an evening. The visit is arranged by the tourist bureau and they try and match up the people according to profession, interests, etc. I spent three days in Beppu by myself, working with a professional basketmaker.

Next we landed in New Zealand, rented a car and drove around both Islands for three weeks. Lots of beautiful scenery, sheep and friendly people. Then onto Fiji and some very theatrical dance performances. I also learned how to make a basket out of one palm leaf. (I'm certain this will be a very important skill in my life). Next, onto Los Angeles and a great visit with Dave's stepbrother Jack and wife Marge and then to San Francisco. I fell in love with San Francisco and intend to revisit. Next Canada and Terra Cotta. I love travel, but home felt very good.

OCTOBER 23, 1985

Dear friends and family,
No, we have not dropped off the end of the earth. Dave arrived back in Lahore in the summer, but I stayed in Canada a couple of extra months and then spent three marvelous weeks traveling through Japan with my friend Beverlee. We lived in Ryokans, visited quiet shrines and gardens and ate beautifully prepared food. Beverlee writes for a food column so we had to photograph and savour every bite. I never thought I would eat raw fish for breakfast, but loved the way it was served.

We revisited Beppu where I spent a few days last year with a basket maker. First, we went into a bamboo forest and thanked the trees for the bamboo I was going to use. I then sat on the floor with my basket master for three days, slicing bamboo very thin to make my basket. My arms and legs were covered with knife cuts and I think he feared for both our lives. This trip I brought him a gift of one of my raku bowls. He was surprised to see me and couldn't stop laughing.

What a contrast to arrive in Pakistan. The first thing I noticed was the intrusion on my privacy. In Japan, no one stares directly at you, whereas here you are on obvious display all the time. Also once again I had to get used to the audio intrusion of the mosque loudspeakers. I swear that on Fridays they have "Tiny Talent" time. You cannot get away from all the squeaky voiced young boys screeching over the speakers, no doubt training for a permanent career. We still have the guy blowing the whistle all through the night to keep the Chokador (the night watchman) awake. Of course he sleeps and we stay awake.

I have been here for two months and have pretty well been chained to the word processor because we have a deadline to get the bids out and then, joy oh joy, we head to Goa Beach for Christmas. I do not want to spend another Christmas here. Each day I frantically type away hoping not to get caught in an instant unannounced power outage. I try to get around this by saving every five minutes. Lahore started its annual load shedding which means that the power can be cut at any time during the day. The Government is trying to save electricity by shutting off the electric power for periods of time. It is like playing Russian roulette. They are supposed to have a schedule and at the moment it seems to be every time I get started. Today we had a total of four hours blackout, two in the morning and two in the afternoon. I don't know how businesses are supposed to operate

In between working I have been gathering bits and pieces together for papermaking and will have something to show for it very shortly. (enshalla, meaning God willing) I had a short get together with Scheherazade who has generously offered to share her pottery studio. It is small and she already shares it with a 103-year-old potter. I wonder if clay acts as a preservative? I said I would go over one day and dig and prepare my clay and see what happens. Meanwhile I am concentrating more on getting started with a paper studio.

Everyday happenings continue to amuse and sometimes even surprise me. This morning I received two welcome letters and decided to sit on the porch as quietly as is possible, have a coffee and enjoy my letters. I was settled for about five minutes when eight men arrived with a large bamboo ladder, plunked it about six feet from where I was sitting and for the next few hours continually climbed up and down with pots of dirt or piles of bricks on their heads. A few days earlier, we had reported to Mrs. Masood that there was a small hole in our roof and some rain was leaking in and staining the walls. "Don't worry," she said, "I will get a man to fix it. It should only take a day and then we can paint your rain stained walls." Well, these eight men descended upon us and proceeded to tear up the entire flat roof, which consisted of two layers of red bricks, plus a thick layer of dirt. It seemed as though each one had been given a sledgehammer and spent about eight hours a day smashing our roof. Two weeks later they left. The roof no longer leaks, but the whole house is now collapsing from all the pounding. Our wall has permanent large cracks running up and down through the rain pattern. Our nonplussed landlady said she would send in the painters and all would be well. When she saw the look of horror on our faces, she said, "We will wait until after Christmas." The last time the painters came, it took an entire week to scrape all the paint off the floors. They don't believe in drop sheets and don't do cleanup.

There is no sign whatsoever of the upcoming Christmas season except for the local choir (for some reason called the International Choir) that sang carols in a Christian church last night. We came home and put on our one and only Christmas tape of White Christmas. Of course we thought it was Bing Crosby, but it turned out to be Elvis Presley. I think we bought it at the duty free while coming through Dubai.

Yesterday Dave and I took some time out to go for a walk early in the morning. We live in a newer area called Gulberg and there is a small park not far away. We are surrounded by large houses, and, much to our astonishment, found our house backs onto a hidden area where a large group of colourful gypsies live in mud huts. We made the discovery this morning when we noticed some of the gypsies in their colourful skirts (quite a contrast to the usual shalwar kameez) walking along the edge of the park and gathering string, grasses, discarded tinfoil etc. and piling it all on top of their heads. We decided to follow them, and this is how we discovered a complex of mud huts with a small herd of water buffalo. They were even more astonished to see us, but friendly and invited us to take many photos. Men were again not allowed to photograph women, so I photographed them while Dave shot the herd, the men and the dwellings. There is no such thing here as zoning, and they were such a delight to come upon. I am just this week starting to get my paper making pulled together and realize I am competing with the gypsies for the raw material of old paper, grasses etc. Pakistan is way ahead of North America when it comes to recycling. A man comes to your house with a little scale and weighs the tin, glass and paper that the cleaner has carefully saved from the garbage. One must be careful what is discarded, because a very private piece of mail could end up being used by market vendors for wrapping foods such as peanuts. I have managed to save two pieces of children's art used by an old lady selling dahl.

Speaking of our area Gulberg, here is an account of a bank near us being "looted." It took the thieves six hours, possibly because they were "feasting" on foreign liquor. What the liquor was doing in the bank is probably another interesting story.

Bank looted in broad daylight

By Our Staff Reporter

LAHORE, Nov. 28: Four smartly-dressed young men broke into Habib Bank ladies branch at Liberty Market in broad daylight on Friday and decamped with jewellery and cash worth lakhs of rupees.

The young dacoits entered the bank forcibly at 9.30 am and injured the watchman, Muhammad Sardar, at gun-point and tied him with plastic ropes, and stayed there for more than six hours.

The dacoits had brought with them modern equipments, including three gas-cylinders, cutter, welding tools and some other devices.

They also feasted themselves with foreign liquor during the robbery. They tried to open the strong room of the bank by their modern equipments and after a few hours they entered the room.

In the strong room the dacoits broken three lockers and carried away jewellery worth lakh of rupees.

Ghulam Hasan, according to gunman of the Bank, the dacoits entered the bank at 9.30 am. A young man in three-piece suit came and told the gunman, Muhammad Sardar who was on duty, that he had brought some bags for the lady Manager of the bank, so the gunman opened the door.

As soon as he opened the door, one dacoit pushed him away and forcibly entered the bank and seized the gunman. Just after three other dacoits, who were sitting in a maroon car rushed into the bank carrying their modern equipments.

The dacoits tried to open the lock of the strong room, but it went out of order and was thus jammed. Later the dacoits tried to break the hinges of iron door of the strong room. They also remained unsuccessful in this effort.

Finally they made a window-like opening from the two and a half inches iron wall from the right side of the strong room.

The dacoits broke the locks of three lockers, 72, 74 and 95 and carried away jewellery from there. They also tried to open lockers, bearing No. 25, 46, 70 and 59 but in vain. They later left bank the at about 4 p.m. The gunman, Muhammad Sardar was released when Ghulam Hasan came to replace him. He immediately informed the police.

The news of the dacoity spread like a jungle fire in Gulberg and ladies who had their lockers at the bank made a beeline to see whether their lockers were saved.

Printed and published for The Nation (Pvt.) Ltd., at NIPCO Press, 4-Shaarey Fatima Jinnah, Lahore, by Majid Nizami.

NOVEMBER 12, 1985

A few weeks have ~~past~~ *passed* since last I wrote. I will get back to the subject of my attempts to get a papermaking studio pulled together. I have never made paper in my life, but once watched a small boy pulling some pulp through a screen at the Toronto Science Center. I thought if a ten- year old can do it, surely so can I. So far I have managed to save all the paper we are using in the computer for recycling and also through the help of a friend at Packages, a large paper container plant, I have managed to get a small amount of refined wood pulp that is sent from Canada.

Collecting the bagasse or sugar cane is another matter. There are small, bright green stands on street corners where the vendor puts whole sugar cane through a press and sells the juice as a very sweet drink. He then discards the crushed cane called bagasse and this is what I need to make the paper. Of course, I needed Qamar for this operation. He asked the vendor if we could have a few bags of his scraps. He was reluctant to give it to us for some reason and wanted to know why we wanted it. Qamar was looking embarrassed, but I told him it was OK to tell the man I was going to cook it up and transform it into paper. Of course we had again drawn our usual crowd, and when Qamar made this pronouncement, they all looked at me as though I was going to momentarily ascend into the Heavens.

Here is a photo of me beside one of the stands. It was published in an article I wrote about my papermaking experiences for the Ontario Crafts Council magazine.

When I was in a small village a couple of weeks ago, I saw a beautiful old primitive cutting machine for cutting corn stalks for cattle feed. I was so excited and asked Qamar to find out where and if I could buy one. Neither one of us uttered a word about what we wanted it for. I am learning. I took a photo and yesterday went again into the old city to the machinery market to try and locate such a cutter. Of course I was not supposed to be there but trooped after Qamar from stall to stall trying to avoid being trampled to death by horse carts, etc. I finally had to give in. No such machinery was to be found. Perhaps I will take my cane and go back to the village and ask the "village cutter" to do the job for me. As you can see, setting up a studio takes a bit of time and determination, but is a marvelous experience. I would suspect that this could be a case where the process of setting up may prove to be more interesting than the finished product.

It has also taken me three trips to the local woodworker to get my mold and deckle made. Even though I gave him a photocopied drawing from a book I found in Canada, the mold was made upside-down. I patiently explained this to Qamar, who patiently translated this into Urdu. It has now been corrected and the carpenter did a great job. This is the same woodworker who made my bed frames for me, so we are now old buddies and no request fazes him.

The head of the Art College is interested in my plans to experiment with indigenous material for the paper and wants to set me up a space at the College. I said I would like to do some uninterrupted work at home first and then in the New Year (enshallah) will spend some time at the college. Now that we have finished the biggest part of the project for this period, I am going to try and do something for my soul and Dave hopes to get working on making technical videos with a Pakistani cohort.

Well, it is time for a couple of snippets. A Pakistani gentleman speaks out bravely against "stoning" and a racket is unveiled, which uses small children for camel racing. Both practices to me are so unthinkable.

Death by stoning

I was horrified beyond measure when the other day I read a news item that a woman charged with adultery has been sentenced to death by stoning.

Here I am reminded of an episode in the life of Jesus Christ. A woman similarly charged was brought before him by his antagnists. Jesus was told of the Mosaic Law which provided death by stoning for a person found guilty of adultery. Jesus was known to be a very compassionate and kind man. And yet he was called upon to uphold this harsh and inhuman law. He was in a quandary. He had earlier declared that his duty was to uphold the laws of Moses and not to break them as was the charge against him by the Senhedrin. And he was also required to uphold human dignity. So he gave the judgment: "Let one who is without sin amongst you cast the first stone." The woman's accusers were, however, men of moral courage. They admitted that they were not without sin and so they left the woman unharmed.

Is anyone amongst us without sin and, therefore, fit to cast the first stone on this condemned Pakistani woman? Have we the moral courage to admit of our sins? Has our march backwards in time begun? If so, then history has no compunction about giving its own verdict.

As one of your worthy correspondents said a few days ago in these columns about the plight of another un-fortunate Pakistani woman and about the apathy which has become a hallmark of our nation; what are our chairpersons, begums, begmat, wazirs doing? Are they free of the Iftar parties to give thought and attention to such trivial affairs as the possible stoning to death of a woman? Where are our leaders who talk so tall about human dignity, the United Nations Charter, about equality of sexes?

ZAHID HUSSAIN BORHANI

Children used in camel races: racket unveiled

By Our Staff Reporter

KARACHI, Sept 15: FIA Immigration authorities offloaded seven children with their six "guardians" before boarding a Dubai-bound aircraft at the Karachi Airport, on Sunday.

All of them were later handed over to FIA (Passport Cell) for establishing if the "guardians" who brought the children from Rahimyar Khan, were genuine relatives or not.

Besides, the FIA is probing as to why the minors whose ages ranges between three to five years, were being taken to Dubai on "employment visa," having been shown as camel riders.

The six male members were identified as Rahim Bux, Mohammad Saleem, Mohammad Yasin, Abdul Majeed, Ikhtiar Ahmad and Bholu Ram.

Preliminary inquiries revealed that the children are used in camel races in UAE by Arabs who pay huge sums for them. The children are tied with the camel's tail and made to run under duress, FIA sources said, adding that details of the racket would be released later.

NOVEMBER 26, 1985

Hello again.

I would love to be able to report that I returned in October to a blissful household where everything was as it should be, but of course this was not so. Our trusty cook George decided to stay working for the slimming clinic where he supposedly went temporarily when we left on our six month hiatus and trip. The owner Mr. James rules the place with an iron fist, and I think George is afraid to leave. Apparently, there is another slimming clinic in town that wants Mr. James out of town, so they are trying to frame him. They spread a rumour that he is giving drugs to women patients as a part of the slimming diet. The rivals, according to the story, then try and slip into the house and plant the alleged drug under the cushions and call the police. One of George's jobs besides cooking for all the staff, is to run around every 10 minutes or so looking for "the stuff." When we left, George only weighed about 110 lbs, but now he is almost a shadow. He came to see Dave before I returned and said he wanted to come back but had to sort some things out. Meanwhile he would send his wife Mercy to do both the cooking and the cleaning.

This was the scene when I arrived. It didn't take long to realize that Mercy did not have a clue how to cook. Dave had been living on fruit and yogurt and saw no problem. I saw a problem and told her she could stay on as a cleaner, but I was hiring a professional cook. When George heard that his gravy train was about to be derailed, he appeared and asked for a bit more time. We gave him two weeks to return and extended Mercy as cook (using the word loosely) until that time. A few days later Mercy came to me and said that she was worried that Mr. James would put a spell on George because George was leaving. I said "Don't be silly, Mr. James cannot cast spells." Well, I may have spoken too soon, because George never appeared, and Mercy, along with some household articles, disappeared.

I must speak to Mr. James and get his formula. We found out yesterday that George has been taking all the money that Mr. James was giving him for groceries and betting on the horses. Obviously his horse did not come in and he was not able to get back into the stores and pay the accounts he was charging. I haven't heard the outcome, but knowing Mr. James, George could easily be behind bars by now. I really liked George in spite of all his many "character deficiencies", and I miss him. He was a good cook and always cheerful.

DECEMBER 19, 1985

Hi once again.

It is another day in sunny Lahore and we have just hired Usaf (also known as Joseph) who can not be described as cheerful, is rather plumpish and theatrical, and makes scrumptious lemon pies. Of course he plays all the tricks that George did, but is not as clever. Or perhaps I am getting a bit wiser. The cooks always record how the shopping money was spent and I usually at least pretend each week to go over the books with scrupulous care. Usaf was very blatant with his overpricing. I suggested to him that the shops were taking advantage of him and I would do the grocery shopping for the next few weeks so I could know how much I had to give him to run the household. As I said, he is very theatrical and he let me know that this was an insult to his integrity. Since then our kitchen and dining room have been the center of much drama. This week, Ross, Dave's boss from Canada arrived in Lahore and seemed to know not to request a big company dinner. I went to the market with Qamar of course and bought a big plump chicken (a rather rare find) and asked Usaf to cook it. He promptly slammed the chicken on the counter and insisted it was not a chicken but a duck. He was upset because he did not buy the bird. I said, "I have cooked for many years in Canada and know a chicken from a duck." Tensions were very high and the only reason he still had a job was because Ross was coming to dinner. I do admit that I both need and love having someone do the cleaning and cooking, but sometimes I wonder if it is worth the emotional strain of trying to keep one step ahead (actually I would settle for only one step behind.)

Here is a photo of the "happy household"taken on our balcony. left to right: honestly can't remember her name, Memsahib Agnes, Usaf, Qamar and Sahib Dave.

The temperature is perfect here now (approx. 70F in the day) and I have again taken up golf to get some air and exercise without a mob around. I still have a pro whom I go around with for the sum of $3.00 for a couple of hours. He is the national golf pro for all of Pakistan and my golfing must drive him crazy. I am also, with reluctance, playing darts. I really do not know what I am doing, but by some fluke last night I won the high single score. I didn't even understand what was happening, but the captain of our team was jumping up and down with glee. I would like to quit while I am ahead, but entertainment of any kind is rare here. I cannot take the game seriously, but Dave does and he is getting quite good at it.

Speaking of entertainment, we went to a Pakistani movie the other night and it was quite an experience. The movie was *Rambo* with Sylvester Stallone. They get mostly action, macho type of movies here. They can't show anyone kissing or touching, but they can see people being punched to pulp. We were told ahead to take earplugs and I wore them for the entire movie.

The part of the evening that I enjoyed most was the one big commercial depicting a typical western bar scene. A very tired, mean looking cowboy slinks into a bar. The crowd looks aghast and everyone steps aside. He saunters up to and pounds on the bar and demands "A package of chips and a Teem." He devours the chips in one handful, chugalugs the soft drink in one gulp and saunters out. No one found this funny except us. It is amazing how much they want to copy even the worst of the western world. Bombay is one of the largest film making cities in the world, but their films by our standards are so sad. They are all a mishmash of novellas. Actresses here are no better than prostitutes on the social scale and I was told that no "good" Pakistani family would allow their sons to marry one.

Another big highlight here is an evening of videos. They are all pirated, but the latest thing is some enterprising person puts a movie camera up to a TV screen and photographs the entire movie. He then sells it to a video shop and dumb people like yours truly rent them. We rented a comedy the other night and whenever a funny line was uttered, we could hear the family laughing and clapping. I guess there is a mike attached to the movie camera that records whatever is happening in the room while the movie is being photographed. One friend said she rented a video where people kept walking in between the TV screen and the movie camera. As a result she kept getting shadows of the people on the screen.

And now for a "snippet" about VCRs and morality.

> **FROM OUR CORRESPONDENT**
>
> SAHIWAL, Aug. 19: There would appear to be no way of stopping people from viewing foreign, often blue, films on the VCR. A very large number of people these days own VCRs and seem to be able to procure video tapes of dubious nature from the market.
>
> Young people in the particular are addicted to the habit of viewing smutty movies, but grown-ups are not lagging far behind. You can often see parents sitting together with their children, viewing films that are far from decent. More often than not, they are third rate sex-crime features.
>
> The cinema business has been virtually ruined. According to exhibitors, it is just not possible to bill good films these days, because no one would come to watch them. And, the movies the cinema-goers want to see are not approved by censors for exhibition.

Besides all this talk about entertainment or lack thereof, I feel that I should give at least a few hours a week to a charitable cause. So far I have visited a school for blind boys. They are being taught to support themselves by caning and weaving. They do a good job. There is also a large movement to help educate women in the villages regarding their rights, but only about 10 percent of the village women are literate. I have read two novels by a Pakistani writer Bepsi Sidwal. Her first is the "Crow Eaters" and her second "The Marriage." The Marriage gives a good account of a young Pakistani girl living in the tribal north and is very enlightening. I recommend them both if you can find them. When I need to quiet my soul (quite often) I go back to Krishnamurti, who now seems like an old friend.

But all of this will soon be behind us for a couple of weeks as we head for Goa Beach. I can hardly wait. We wish all of you a very happy, healthy and fulfilling Christmas and New Years and a wonderful 1986.

Here are a couple of "snippets" about education for women.

Vocational institute for women

FROM OUR CORRESPONDENT

HAFIZABAD, Oct. 19: A vocational institute has been set up at Hafizabad for which the Government has already procured equipment worth Rs. 1.50 lakh.

Initially, the institute is to be housed at a rented premises, but subsequently it will have a building of its own. The requisite funds for this purpose have been allocated in the current year's budget.

Training in knitting, sewing and other related vocations will be imparted to women in order to enable them supplement their incomes to lead respectable lives. Poor and destitute women will be paid a monthly stipend of Rs. 100 during the training.

Nawaz asks lady MPAs to promote education

The Punjab Chief Minister, Mr. Nawaz Sharif, has called upon the lady MPAs to play their role in the promotion of education in order to improve literacy rate in the province.

He was talking to a delegation of lady MPAs attending the current session of the Punjab Assembly, on Tuesday.

Mr. Nawaz Sharif said the ladies had to perform an important role in national development. As such they should make suggestions for welfare of the people particularly for the women folk. He said the nation cannot progress without promoting literacy and without improving the standard of education. The women, he added, owed this responsibility to the nation to educate their children and make concerted efforts for the promotion of education, diffusion of knowledge and moral re-armament of the society.

1986 LETTERS

February 2, 1986
50-G Gulberg 111
LAHORE, PAKISTAN
Phone 872711 (when it works)

Hi Everybody,
This is my very first letter of the year and it finds us back in Pakistan. We did manage to get to Goa Beach for Christmas and loved it. We had a special Christmas dinner set up on the beach with a main dish of shark in an amazing sauce wrapped in banana leaves. It was a late meal and there was a full moon and a warm breeze coming off the ocean. Before dinner we attended a Christmas Eve Service in a magnificent old Cathedral and listened to the choir sing carols in Hindustani. "Silent Night" in Hindustani is very beautiful, but a bit weird to my Anglo ears.

On Christmas day we decided to have a small cocktail party on our little front patio.

We decorated the flowering shrubs outside our unit, hung paper lanterns with candles in them, and then went around to all of the other units in the hotel and invited whoever was there to come and join us. We ended up with five families including a bunch of kids who devoured the Christmas pudding we had purchased from a nearby city. It was really fun because we had families from Sweden, France, England and the United States.

After two weeks of lazing around in the sun and touring the nearby local villages, we reluctantly dragged ourselves away and headed for North Western India and for the camel safari that we had promised ourselves from the year before. We took a long, arduous train ride to Jaisalmere, a magnificent old city in the Indian desert near the Pakistan Border. It was like taking a trip in a time machine back a thousand years into a storybook land. Jaisalmere is a huge fortress and castle perched 250 feet up on what looks like a gigantic anthill. The city dates back to Alexander the Great and was on the Old Silk Route. It hasn't changed much since those times and because it is so remote, it really hasn't been inundated as yet by masses of tourists. The fortress encircles the city and contains a fantastic old castle as part of the fortress wall. The city core is a meandering series of narrow cobblestone streets lined with magnificent old sandstone buildings, which are adorned with intricate stone carvings and stone lacework. Most of the structures are in excellent repair and in the evening desert sun, they glow a honey colour, thus the name the "Golden City." We managed to get a room on the roof of the old castle, which afforded us a breathtaking view of the surrounding desert and the inner city. We sat there in the evening and witnessed the sun set into a pool of gold.

After much searching, we purchased a charming old hanging quilt with appliquéd and stitched designs depicting the early culture of Rhajastan. All the bargaining left us feeling rather hungry, so we wended our way past the many holy cows that seemed to own the streets and finally selected a small restaurant where a buffet of local foods held our interest. We sat at a long table next to a couple of travelers, and, as seems natural when traveling, started up a conversation without benefit of introductions. We mentioned that the area fascinated us and reminded us a bit of the small Greek island of Skyros that we had visited years back. The lady's face beamed as she informed us they were from Skyros. It turned out that her husband was educated at McGill University in Montreal. We had a wonderful evening of conversation and good food. When they heard that we were in search of a camel safari, they suggested we go to a small village called Kuri, approximately a two hour bus drive further into the desert, and take the safari from there.

After a few days of resting and meandering, we took a decrepit old bus loaded with three times the passengers for which it was designed and headed further into the desert to Kuri. When we reached the village we were immediately surrounded by many curious villagers and were treated to a great lunch in one of the mud huts. We arranged for two camels to take us on a three-day safari further into the desert to some remote settlements. The owner and a young boy accompanied us. Getting up on the camel proved to be quite a feat. Camels have a most peculiar manner of getting up onto all fours. The long back legs go up first and I felt for sure that I was going to be catapulted over its head. I held on for dear life thinking that maybe I would just not get off the camel again for the entire three days.

I could not believe how high up I was and tried to hold on and get balanced as the camel took off in the most uncoordinated gait you can imagine. Once underway, it settled into a more rhythmic motion that was quite pleasant, sort of like being in a moving rocking chair. They have the unpleasant habit of burping and you can only hope that the breeze, if there is one is, blowing away from you. Along the way, we met many gazelle gracefully foraging on the sparse vegetation, desert foxes looking for their feed of mice, monstrous hawks and incredible vultures. We happened upon a camel that had recently expired, and the vultures were standing in a circle around the carcass waiting for a couple of dogs to finish. What an amazing sight– sort of a grotesque formal dinner party.

The silence of the desert has to be experienced to appreciate its impact. To witness a breathtaking desert sunset while riding along swaying back and forth to the slow rhythmic gait of the camel, is to know true contentment. This was one of the most spiritual experiences of my life.

Our guide, it turned out, had an incredible voice and occasionally he would break the silence by suddenly bursting into song. I am sure his rich voice could be heard for miles across the desert. We traveled on for some time into the night with only a sliver of moon in a sky filled with brilliant stars. Earlier in the afternoon, we stopped under a very welcome tree, and enjoyed the shade and the tea that was brewed on a small fire consisting of a few twigs. Eventually, we reached a tiny village where the only sign of life was the barking of dogs. A lone figure approached us and our guide spoke to him. A mud and grass hut was vacated and arranged for us for the night for the sum of 10 rupees. ($1.00) The young boy prepared a fire on the floor of the hut between the two charpoys, which would be our beds for the night. (Sorry Mrs. Masood, but I finally got to sleep on a charpoy.) It was quite chilly by now, and we were informed the temperature sometimes drops to freezing at this time of year. A meal of chapattis, dhal, onions, eggplant and goat was prepared for us. It sounds better than it tasted, but was washed down with some desert wine, a quite tasty local fermentation made from the cactus plant.

The next morning we rose for an early morning meditation while watching the sunrise over the village. Our guide knelt on a mat for his Call to Prayer. With a feeling of peacefulness and gratitude we headed off for another day. This was without doubt another of life's incredible experiences.

MARCH 21, 1986

Happy Spring Equinox to everyone.

Back in Lahore things are quiet. The bid evaluations for Dave's job are all completed and have been sent to the Asian Development Bank for their final approval before purchases are made. This has been a very big contract and several large companies are bidding. By the time the purchase orders are made up and sent out and the equipment arrives here, it will be September. Dave's contract runs out at the end of October, so they are looking into a six month extension which would mean being here until the end of April 1987.

Taking advantage of the quiet time, I have spent some time making paper. I rather enjoy the fact that I don't know what I am doing. It is very freeing, and since no one else here knows either, who can say what I am doing isn't the correct way. I am making all the paper out of sugar cane and combining it with banana pulp. I only have one blender in the house and I refuse to go to the duty free to buy another one (remember the toaster), so I share this with the cook and also cook my pulp in the kitchen. Not the best arrangement, but all I have. I can't believe it, but next week I am giving a workshop at the National College of Art on Handmade Paper. This really takes nerve considering I am such a neophyte in this field, and I have had a few sleepless nights thinking about it. It is getting warm now and my converted bathroom/studio is becoming a Mecca for mosquitoes. Every day Long Suffering Usaf puts his nose in the air and runs in with a bug spray. Supplies of bagasse, banana pulp and many grasses are starting to pile up and I have taken over one of the outdoor rooms in the servants' quarters for storage. I am thankful we have no live-ins because I really do need this extra space.

MARCH 26, 1986

It is a few days later and another "studio incident" has taken place. Qamar recently helped me collect some old banana tree stems that had been thrown beside the streets waiting for the gypsies or whoever gets there first to pick them up for further use. I asked him to watch out for more stems and yesterday he arrived with a 12-foot banana tree on the car top carrier of our little Nissan Sunni. It took us days to chop the stem up and another day to straighten out the huge dent in the carrier. I can now see that I have to be careful what I ask for.

A side effect of all our trips with Qamar has been that he has "seen the light," creatively speaking. Before on car trips, Dave would suddenly call out, "Stop here for a minute Qamar while I get a few photos." or I would screech "Stop, Qamar." and go running off into the fields startling a group of farmers as I gathered rice and wheat grasses for my paper. Now, without even asking, he keeps pulling the car over and says "Look, see, making baskets." It now takes us about half a day to go 20 kms., but it's fun.

I went over to the College last week to talk about my workshop and lucked into a series of three lectures given by a remarkable art historian from Sri Lanka. She is currently teaching at Yale and has lived, taught, painted and danced in Paris, Istanbul and Tokyo, to name a few places. She gave two one-hour lectures without benefit of a note. I was impressed. She spoke on the Role of the Creative Artist and also on Religion and the Arts. What also impressed me is that she dropped in out of the blue and said, "I will be in Lahore for a few days and would like to talk to your students if you want me to." The College has literally no funding so they were thrilled to have such a knowledgeable woman offer her services free of charge.

We are in a slow period here at work, and have some time to golf. Dave tried it but gave up in complete frustration after he lost four balls in one day. I even entered a tournament and had the honour of coming in last. The best part is that I don't care. I just go out for the exercise and the space. The weather was in the high70s, but this week dipped to 70. All the trees are in bloom, and outside the window at this moment, is a beautiful huge tree laden with what look like white orchids. It is called a Frangipani and has the most luxurious scent. The local people eat the buds in a curry dish. I tasted it last week – very good. Our small porch now hosts all sorts of plants that we bought from an American leaving for home. We soon realized that they were dying so hired a part time 80-year-old moli (gardener). The nicest benefit is that he gardens for a very wealthy family and two or three times a week brings me the most beautiful bouquets of roses, exotic plants, etc. Of course I love him. Not only does he bring me flowers, but also he has a very gentle nature.

Last week Lahore hosted the big annual Horse and Cattle show. It lasts one week and we witnessed horse dancing, camel racing, motorcycle leaping, marching bands and native dancing (all men of course) in very colourful costumes. I can only say it was spectacular. We were kindly given seats in the VIP section for the night performance, all performed by torchlight. The Pakistani people, when they revert to old colonial customs, are more British than the British. Waiters wearing tall bright turbans constantly served food and hot tea in china teacups up and down the aisles. This was only in the VIP section, which held hundreds of people.

A couple of weeks ago, we drove to Multan in the south of Pakistan, a five hour drive. This is where Dave's mother was born. Her father was in the British army and stationed there.

Multan is the oldest city in southeast Asia and is noted for its many Sufi shrines and its historic blue and white pottery. We were disappointed to find only a few pottery shops. We did manage to meet one ancient man making tiles in the traditional manner. His family had been making similar tiles for 800 years. He allowed us to photograph him working in a room about the size of a small closet and with only outdoor light. I want to show these photos to potters in Canada so they can realize how fortunate they are to have good, well lit, studio space.

We also visited the small city of Uch, one of the early centers for religious retreats that was built in approximately 325 B.C. Here we found an ancient banyan tree in the middle of a small courtyard and were told by the local residents that many early religious leaders had visited and sat and prayed under this very tree. Nearby is Harrappa, the cradle of Indus civilization with several 5000 year old ruins.

It is snippet time, with an interesting article from a Pakistani woman speaking out against a "disgraceful practice" and then the four basics by Dr. Lall.

Disgraceful practice

THE MEN of Pakistan have no shame, nor can they call themselves true Muslims! As long as they disrobe, relieve themselves and "clean" themselves in public or allow other men to do so, they have no shame and do not believe in modesty and cleanliness, which are enjoined on all true Muslims.

Don't tell me these men are poor, illiterate villagers who don't know better! There are many homeless women living all about our city, and I have never once seen any one relieving herself within sight of public places, or returning from the bushes holding up her kameez and tying her shalwar! If the mothers, wives, sisters and daughters of these men do not expose themselves, why do these men? More importantly, why don't the good men admonish these "kafirs" and send them to the nearest mosque (there is always a mosque within a few minutes walk) to use the toilets? Why hasn't there been a cry of outrage heard across the land calling for landlords and shopkeepers to supply public toilets? All neighbourhood stores have water and electricity within the large towns and cities. These people make lakhs of rupees, yet promote filth, disease, death and anti-Islamic practices by sending the common working man into the streets to relieve themselves.

For God's sake, do something about this disgrace! —MRS. A.T. SIDDIQI, Islamabad.

The four basics

NOW THAT limited political activity has been restored and all parties are politicking vigorously, one gets the impression from newspapers that everyone is trying to project what is good for the people and how it can be achieved. However I feel that the basic principles have not been identified by any one. These need to be identified before plans etc, can be made for the good of the people in Pakistan.

Recently I was presented a nice book and I find these basic principles very well-defined in it. For the information of your readers I may note them down here:

i) Freedom of worship, (ii) Freedom of speech, (iii) Freedom from hunger and (iv) Freedom from fear. —Dr. ERNEST LALL, Taxila.

APRIL 4, 1986

I pulled myself out of bed at 6.a.m. this morning and waved good-bye to Dave as he left to go wild boar hunting with the scruffiest group of locals I have yet to see. He had mentioned one day that he would like to try it, and good old Qamar said, "I arrange, Sahib." These comrades are all friends and relatives of Qamar. More about this later.

I have given my seven-day work shop at the Art College and am happy and relieved to say that all went well. I am not mainly interested in paper for printmaking, but that is what they wanted to do. I worked with small groups of four female students with many observers throughout the day. The atmosphere was relaxed, much like Sheridan where I studied, so I felt very much at home. We made many large sheets of paper, awaiting a work shop with a visiting printmaker from Britain, Bartolomeu Dos Santos. He is the head of the printmaking department at Slade. I am going to attend his first workshop tomorrow as an observer. He will go through all the steps of etching and will use our handmade paper for printing. I will pray (to whomever) that the paper holds together and takes a good print.

The school itself is unique in Pakistan and is divided into three areas: 1. Design - photography, ceramics, textile printing and weaving. 2. Fine Arts - basic foundation, painting, printmaking and sculpture. 3 - Architecture. They have never offered papermaking before, so I don't know where that would fit in. I enclose a photo of me and the class, all girls except for the technician.

APRIL 18, 1986

It is now a couple of weeks later and I am so happy and elated to tell you that I had the privilege of meeting Mother Theresa. She is very small and looks like a little walking tea towel. She dresses in a white sari with a blue border covering her head as well, exactly like the tea towels my grandmother used. She visited an orphanage in Lahore and spoke to a small group of us. Her speech was short, but you could feel her sense of faith and love. Her voice is very soft and her visit was treated with the reverence due to her. You could hear a pin drop.

She told about an incident that had occurred earlier in the year while she was at her home base in Calcutta. A man came, asking her to fill a prescription for his baby who was very ill. People donate all their left-over drugs to her mission and she has the authority to distribute them. She had to tell this man that they could not help him because they did not have the needed drug. At that moment, a man walked in with a basketful of drugs he had collected and right on top was the needed medicine in exactly the correct amount. By the time she finished the story, I had tears running down my face. To be in her presence is a remarkable experience and if I had had a thousand dollars to give her at that moment, I would gladly have done so.

I am enclosing two photos of Mother Theresa in the center of the book.

It is late and time to end this letter, but first I want to tell you the outcome of Dave's boar hunt. He will never again mention wanting to go boar hunting. It turns out that they chased a wild boar for miles across country. All the guys were much younger than Dave, but of course he could not admit that, and felt he had to keep up with them. They practically had to carry him into the house. He strained his back, and days later, it still hurts. Of course the boar was eventually hunted down and killed and butchered and each participant was to get his share. Well, we came home on a Saturday night to find the following note from Qamar on the windshield of the car. He had Sunday off. We could not quite decipher it and am copying it here as a test of your skills.

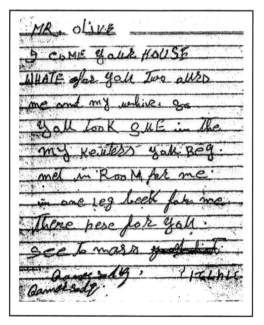

Give up? I still cannot give a literal translation, but what it said was that he came to our house and waited for two hours, he and his wife ... The wild pig is in our trunk and he took one leg ... and these here are for you. See you tomorrow. Qamar Sadiq.

We spent ages trying to translate this and of course knew nothing about the pig being delivered. We could not understand it at all and didn't really worry about it. When Qamar came to work Monday we discovered that the wild pig that was for Dave was in the trunk of the poor little Nissan. You can imagine the smell in all that heat. Of course we had to get rid of the pig and almost had to get rid of the Nissan. We kept Qamar.

Speaking of Qamar, here is another note, wherein he must go to his village because his mother's sister is dead. One veteran Memsahib told me that when she hired new staff, she took down the names of their relatives and checked them off as they died. When they ran out of relatives, that was the end of the holidays.

MAY 7, 1986

Hi friends
Guess what! Our stay has been extended until mid April, 1987. We are arriving back in Canada July 10 for approximately 18 days to try and rent our house and extend the contract on my studio/gallery at the Forge. On June 12, we are taking a jaunt over to Nairobi from Karachi to visit with Bob and Jo. This does not leave us much time at home, but we want to take the opportunity to visit Nairobi while they are there. We have to rent our Terra Cotta house because Steve and Natalie have bought a town house in Streetsville. Mike finishes this year at the School of Design and Caron finishes her first year at Guelph University in International Studies. Many changes have taken place.

Meanwhile, back in good old Lahore, our domestic daily life is about the same as usual. Usaf, our cook hasn't shown up for 10 days, our cleaning lady Alice disappeared for a couple of days because she was run down by a scooter and our phone hasn't worked for five days. I am relieved to report that Alice was not seriously hurt. You may be asking why in the world are we accepting an extension. First of all Dave wants to and has to see the project to a finish. The truth is that we are enjoying life here with quite a few excursions out to try and keep our sanity. The services I will miss are:

1. My once-a-week massages for $1.30.

2. Having someone do all the cleaning (when she shows up).

3. Having someone do all the cooking (when he shows up)

4. Having someone do all the washing and ironing once a week for $13.00 a month.

5. Having a driver to take me anywhere in the car.

All of these services are accompanied with much drama and many headaches but definitely worth it. As you can see I have become LAZY.

MAY 12, 1986

Hi again,
One of the big plusses of living here is the location and opportunity for traveling on short trips. Last week we took advantage of a three day weekend by adding a couple more days and heading into the Northern Frontier and the Swat Valley. We drove to Islamabad and then took a short flight. The Valley is nestled in the Hindu Kush mountains and is called the Switzerland of Pakistan. The air is clean and cool which makes it pleasant for hiking and visiting the many archaeological sites. It is truly a magnificent country with many fruit trees and pine forests, a legacy from the British.

I have no idea what the press is saying about the Libya situation, but thought we should let you know that although things are rather intense here at the moment, we are not in danger. We are using a bit more caution than usual because there is currently a strong anti-American feeling here and of course we are taken as Americans. We have a Canadian flag pasted on the back of our car but have heard that Canada along with Britain approved of Reagan's move, so the flag won't do us much good. In Lahore this week a few processions were taken out (a Pakistan terminology) in which Reagan was burned in effigy. A few American flags were burned and thrown over the wall into the American Center. Rocks were also thrown through the windows at the American Express office and the place was looted. The police intervened, but everyone is staying rather low for a while. Of course, we can't get any real news about the situation and have to be very careful what we say or write. The situation here is very volatile also because Benazir Bhutto, who is running for president, arrived last week and was met by a following of from 50,000 upwards depending where you read about it. One of the slogans on the road was "Down with Americans" and again a few American flags were burned. We happened to be down town in the middle of Benazir Bhutto's parade and got some pictures of her and the crowd. Americans were told to stay off the streets, but I would not have missed the experience of the energy of that crowd. Of course busloads of villagers are given all sorts of perks to come into the city, and they were yelling out support. Some one yelled at me "Go home, go home, we are against Americans." At the same time, a Pakistani man kindly helped me stand on a box so I could more clearly see the procession.

Also last week Agatha Barbara, the president of Malta, paid a visit, and we witnessed her entrance to the Hilton hotel. Approximately a hundred small girls dressed in the various tribal costumes of all the outlying areas of Pakistan, lined the street. There was a band on the roof waiting to play the Malta national anthem. I love a band and waited patiently in the heat for the ceremony to begin. When they started to play, I looked quickly for a way out. The sound was awful and good old Agatha never even flinched. It sounded as though they were all playing a different tune at the same time. The real reason we were present is that we were swimming at the hotel. We looked like something dragged out of a swamp. When Agatha arrived, there was a thick red carpet lined not only by the little girls, but also by representatives from all the consulates and the prime minister of the Punjab. Only Zia was missing. And there we stood Dave and I. My hair was soaking wet from swimming, so I had it shoved up under my hat. I was wearing an old baggy shirt and of course very loose slacks and Dave looked no better. The only reason we were not carted away is that we are foreigners and the hotel has been trained to treat all foreigners politely (even if they do look like bums).

We also took part in another cultural ceremony, Mrs. Masood's grandson's first birthday party. It took place on the back lawn, and is considered to be a most important occasion. It was family only, and consisted of approximately 100 people. The women sat in a circle on straight back chairs on the back lawn and the men mingled with men on the front lawn. When food was finally served, the men came to the back and we were actually allowed to eat and talk together. With the exception of a few very progressive and interesting women in Lahore, it is difficult for me to converse with them in such a large gathering. The educated women speak perfect English, but they usually tend to stick together and are a little shy of foreigners. It was very hot (98F) and I was glad when the party was over. This usually takes place when all the food is eaten.

I just thought of another little domestic note. Last week we let Long Suffering Joseph out of his misery. We have wanted to replace him, but couldn't find an excuse until he didn't show up for ten days. It was so hard for both Dave and me. We are such pussycats, but he had been making our lives as miserable as possible, so I guess I could more accurately say that we let Joseph out of "our" misery. He would serve dinner and stand there with his hat on ready to leave as if we should gulp down our food so he could leave. He was very rude to friends, etc.; however, we waited until he didn't show up for the ten days and decided to take the bull by the horn. It was the strangest conversation.

We told him to come sit with us on the porch, that we wanted to talk to him. We said, "Joseph, we have to let you go because you are arrogant and you insult our guests." The look on his face revealed that he did not understand arrogant. So we carried on. "Joseph, arrogant means that you are rude. You are rude to us and rude to our friends." He pulled himself up to his full height and said, "I will call my lawyer. You cannot fire me." We said "Joseph, that is what we mean by arrogant." Of course he tried to walk off with half our kitchen claiming he had brought all the pots and pans, etc., but we stayed at the door of the kitchen until he left. I wish I weren't such a disaster in the kitchen. I would do without a cook, but you haven't lived until you have tried to cook with an antique Pakistani manufactured stove. Within a day, we hired a new cook, Martin, who is partially deaf and can't seem to remember very much, but he has a much more pleasant personality than Joseph.

MAY 17, 1986

Hello my friends,
We are now in the middle of Ramadan when all good Muslims do not partake of food or drink from approximately 3 a.m. until 7 p.m. This goes on for one month and everyone looks a little dazed as they move around. To make matters more difficult we are in the low 100sF. and the heat just frazzles us. We swim at the Hilton every day. We want to get into some form of fitness and the only exercise one can survive in this weather is in the water. The hotel actually cools the pool through some sort of refrigeration. I don't pretend to understand it, but am truly grateful.

I got a note a few days ago from Martin telling me he was going to lunch and that the dobi might come at 3 p.m. if the water is nice. Other and dobi is no come. As you can see he is the most literate and tells me he can read recipes. We shall see!

AUGUST, 1986

Hi Everyone,

I have no idea what the exact date is. I do know that I have been back in Pakistan approximately four or five days, and it seems like years. I have problems equating time according to minutes, hours, days, etc. It should be measured by intensity of time and these past few days have indeed been intense for reasons such as jet lag, intense humid heat, the Pakistan telephone system, the loss of a new set of golf clubs at Heathrow, a lost handbag at Karachi airport and lost servants...not to mention lost causes.

I am going to try and write a recap from day one, which might slowly help me regain my lost mind. We arrived via British Airlines from London to Karachi at 3:30 a.m., an hour late because some passengers were lost (that word again) and the plane could not take off until they were located and safely belted into their seats.

In Karachi we collected our luggage except for my golf clubs, which did not appear on the conveyer belt. Eventually a British Airlines representative came over, asked to see our tickets and informed us that the clubs were not sent on from Heathrow Airport, but would be forwarded later to us in Lahore via Pakistan Airlines. However, we were advised to check again before we flew out later that morning. In typical Pakistan fashion, we spent the next hour filling out an "A" form to enable the clubs to come through customs. Next we filled out a very long "missing luggage report" Finally, at 5:30 a.m., we dragged our weary bones and tons of cases onto the platform. We were greeted by an onslaught of a dozen porters attempting to push the loaded cart and several taxi drivers frantically trying to pull us into their cabs.

We arrived at the Midday Airport Hotel and collapsed until

11 a.m. when we had to again head for the airport and on to Lahore. While Dave was checking us through, I headed for a small room "For Ladies Traveling Alone in Need of Help." I wasn't alone, but I sure needed help to locate British Airways and enquire if my clubs had been located. I was allowed to use the office phone and was told to my dismay that the clubs were not as yet located, but when they were (enshallah) they would be sent to Lahore via Dubai. In my haste to catch up with Dave and the departing plane, I left my small black purse in the Distress Center. It was not until I was on the plane that I noticed it missing and then couldn't remember if I had it at the airport or had left it at the hotel. I was definitely flipping out. It is amazing how too little sleep and hot humid weather can affect you.

We arrived at Lahore Airport, again fought frantically through the maze of porters and drivers, and after much haggling over the price, rode home in a taxi that would not be allowed on the road in Canada. We were unfortunately not able to contact Qamar to meet us.

When we finally arrived home, I took a deep breath and decided to try to phone the hotel in Karachi in search of my missing handbag. This was a momentous and probably foolish decision, because if anything in Pakistan will test your patience, it is the telephone system. After many unsuccessful attempts to get through, I called 103, supposedly the number for enquiries. I was accustomed to Ma Bell in Canada, who impersonally, but immediately gives you the requested number, (and in many cases now it is done electronically.) But, today when I dialed, and asked for the hotel number, a female voice said "Gee, are you a foreigner?" In the background I could hear many voices laughing and shouting. "Yes," I replied and "From what country?" she asked. I had no idea what this had to do with telephone information, but replied "Canada." "Just a minute." A few seconds later I heard her yell into the babble of noise

"There is a foreign lady on the phone who wants the number for the Midway Hotel." I was a little shocked by the informality of it all, but relieved when she gave me the information. This time a man answered and when I gave the number, he replied "Yes, my dear." I kept thinking, this phone system is probably among the worst in the world, but it sure is friendly. In fact it is so friendly that you seldom have the line to yourself, but share it with another couple equally attempting to have a conversation at the same time. I hung up and in a few minutes the phone rang and my call was put through. Not bad.

Sometimes it can take all day or many days. I was cut off three times, but eventually the hotel found someone who spoke English and I poured out my long, sad story of a missing purse. There was a long pause and then a very confused woman informed me that this was not a hotel, but an industrial building. At this point, my frustration level was so high that I was half crying and half laughing. I reminded myself that patience and a strong sense of humour were called for and poured myself a tall, cold drink. After many more attempts I finally did reach the hotel and was told the Lost and Found had just closed and I would have to call the next day. I began to understand why so many Pakistanis put everything in the hands of Allah. I did that, and Allah came through with flying colours.

The next morning Pakistan Airlines called to say they had found my purse at the airport and were sending it on the next flight to Lahore. Dave agreed that this was indeed a miracle and it would be even a greater one if the contents were all there. His faith is a little shakier than mine. I have also had a guardian angel all my life whose only job is to find and return to me all my lost handbags. I guess she and Allah got together on this one because the purse was intact with all my money and two watches. That very day I wrote a letter to Top Management and brought to their attention the honesty of the staff at Pakistan Airlines. It is now a week later and I still do not have my golf clubs. Yesterday was Independence Day and the next two days are Big Eid, so not much is being accomplished in that direction.

We gave ourselves a couple of days of quiet and then decided it was time to call Qamar, Alice, Martin, the Dobi and the Moli back to work. Dave called the magic number that was to beckon Qamar, who would round up the rest of the crew. This resulted in a very garbled message to Qamar's neighbour who owned the phone. Three days later, and still no Qamar. Finally, in desperation, we called on Mrs. Masood to assist us in Urdu. She called and was told that the neighbour was no longer speaking to Qamar or his family and would not relay the message. We had no idea how to find him, but luckily, that afternoon he appeared and the next morning the whole tribe arrived. Confusion reigned for the rest of the day.

The day after we arrived, August 10, we celebrated our 29th anniversary. We got out a bottle of champagne I had won in a raffle a year earlier, drank a toast to another year of togetherness, and went to the American Club for dinner.

I almost forgot. We stopped over in London on the way back to see my group Raku Exhibition. It felt so strange to be looking at my own work in a foreign gallery, but it was exciting. One British gentleman had left me a note saying "Only a potter from Terra Cotta, Canada could make such fun pots and I wish you a wonderful life." Such a nice note and it made me feel good. The show will travel on to Norway before returning to Canada.

The next night we were slowly unwinding with a cup of after dinner coffee when Max and Maibrit arrived and said, "Come on, we have arranged to go to the Dancing Girls tonight." Since we have been trying to plan this for two years, tired as we were, off we set out at 11:30 p.m. to the Famous Red Light Section of the Old City to see the Famous Dancing Girls. Max had brought along a bachelor friend who supposedly knew where to go and what to do. We were completely ignorant of what to expect, and most Muslim residents don't even admit that this area exists.

We all piled into our little Nissan and arrived at an area swarming with men walking the dirt streets, music blaring and small rooms facing the streets with two or three girls sitting on chairs or couches. Many of the buildings were two or three stories, and girls and old women sat or leaned over the upstairs balconies. The rooms all seemed to consist of a couple of couches and bright overhead lights. They were attached like cages in a zoo with a heavy metal door instead of bars. The doors were left open to show the wares and then tightly closed when the dancing began. Many curious eyes followed us as we were led along the street by our friend to a small room where he conversed with an old woman.

After some negotiation, he told us to come in. The windowless room, which was approximately nine feet by twelve feet, was inhabited by three men with musical instruments sitting on the floor in one corner, and an old woman and a young rather attractive plumpish girl sitting on the floor in another corner. Two dancers stood up to welcome us. The night was hot and humid and the room crowded and stifling once the steel door was clamped shut. I wondered where all this famous dancing was supposed to take place. Max and his friend sat on a couch, Maibrit and I on another equally dilapidated two -seater, and Dave stood behind us in a corner ready to record the activities on our new VCR. I do not think many women attend these evenings and in fact probably none. As it turned out, the dance could have been staged anywhere in public outside of Pakistan. The dancers were dressed in the traditional shalwar kameez, the same type as worn by all Pakistani women everyday in the markets. This consists of a long pair of fully gathered pants, covered to the knees with a straight dress. One of the dancers' kameez was sleeveless, which is unusual. However, they both also wore the dapattas, long scarves that are draped around the neck, shoulders and sometimes the head. It was all very prim and proper and certainly no competition for Bangkok. The dancers attached a pair of "spats" covered with bells to their ankles, the musicians started playing and the girls twirled and sang. The dances were very reminiscent of folk dances of many countries and would have been marvelous if performed in an open field with the tinkling of the bells adding a joyous accompaniment.

They were not what I expected in the "Brothel" area. The music was much too loud and the dance too physical for a small hot room. Perspiration was running off the dancer's foreheads' and in the middle of the dance, a warm soft drink (7-Up) was brought into the room from outside and handed around to us by one of the dancers. The knowledgeable bachelor, our mentor for the evening, handed out some large rupee notes to one of the musicians and in return received bundles of neatly stacked 1-R notes. He then held a few notes to Max's cheek and a dancer came over and plucked it away, at the same time giving the cheek a pinch, very, very risqué. Next he took a portion of the bundle of money and threw it up in the air where, with the help of the overhead fan, it dispersed and fell in a cascade on the heads of the dancers and eventually the floor. We were then each handed a stack of notes and encouraged to follow suit. More money was given to be exchanged, cheeks were pinched, money was thrown in the air in supposed gay abandonment and I kept thinking the scenario was ridiculous.

An old man, who seemed to appear out of nowhere, kept crawling around on the floor scooping up the money while the girls jumped and twirled. Mercifully, because of the heat, we stayed only half an hour. When we were leaving, our mentor spoke to one of the girls and gave her a card with his hotel address.

He was hiring her to come and dance personally for him. He had already handed out approx Rs-800. Along with Max and Dave's Rs300 each, it came to a total of Rs-1400. This is equivalent to a month's salary for a professional cook/bearer. How much, I wondered, did men spend when they are there for the usual two hours. The girls, the band, the old man, the old woman and the young girl all bid us goodbye as though we had just been to their house for a friendly visit, and we were of course invited to come back again. They were much richer and all looked very amused.

OCTOBER 13, 1986

HAPPY CANADIAN THANKSGIVING! We had forgotten that this beautiful day existed until we got a call from a fellow Canadian who invited us over for a "Black Market" turkey dinner, complete with dressing. It was so great. It made me homesick.

Now I want to tell you about another wonderful four-day trip to Skardu in Northern Pakistan in the Himalayas. We completely relaxed and hiked and read and ate (rotten food). The scenery was breathtakingly beautiful with a view of the snow-capped mountains surrounding our cabin. We flew out in a 20 seater Fokker Friendship aircraft, which has a limited flying altitude because it is not pressurized. We had to fly below the cloud level through the mountain passes and in along the beautiful valleys in order to get to Skardu. It was a most spectacular flight. We had purchased a new Video camera so had fun taking pictures of some villagers. Dave was able to let them look into the mini viewer and see themselves, which of course they thought was magic. I bought a large old gathering basket that ties on your back for carting wood and I wore it for about two miles back to the cabin. I wore the strap across my forehead as I often saw the women do. Enroute we met some women who use this basket everyday for carrying wood. They thought it amusing that I was wearing it and stopped to chat with us and mostly giggle. I had quite a time convincing the airline to let me take it back in the tiny plane.

Purchasing the basket was quite a learning experience. After I made my request to buy it, the people of the village had a meeting to decide if they wanted to sell it. Very few foreigners had been to this remote village and I realized how important it was that this negotiation seemed both friendly and fair. A spokesman eventually came to me and said they had decided to sell it and told me a price, which I considered fair to both of us. I have been collecting baskets from different parts of the world for many years and I have been asked to give a slide presentation on "Baskets of Asia" when I return to Canada. This will be a great addition.

I had heard there was great fishing in a small lake in the mountains, but of course I did not have a fishing pole. I bought some line and a couple of hooks and the cook gave me a couple of pieces of raw mutton. Dave and I and an American couple who were trekking took off on a three-mile hike to this lake. It was so peaceful and serene to follow the river with its huge multicoloured rocks and small hand built rope bridges. We were in the middle of NOWHERE and had only a handful of small children following us and then dropping away. I remarked on how quiet and peaceful it was with no one around as I sat down beside a fast running stream and baited my hook. That piece of mutton had not hit the water before an old man appeared out of the clouds carrying a huge ledger. I thought it must be Saint Peter. He asked to see my fishing license. I was so shocked that I just stared at him in disbelief. It seems (so I was informed) that not only was I breaking the law by fishing without a license, but also because I was using mutton as bait. I dug my heels in and absolutely refused to buy his expensive license for just a piece of line and hook and told him so. I then very dramatically rolled up my line and put it away. He hung around for a long time watching us and finally moved on.

Next on our venture a young man in his early twenties joined us. He was studying for a degree through the mail and desperately wanted to practice his limited English. He asked us to look at a lesson that was giving him problems. It was an English lesson and was all about comparisons and contrasts and he had to describe "shoes." He had to compare and contrast the shoes using style, colour, etc. It was the weirdest assignment, and there we sat on a grassy hill overlooking a magnificent turquoise lake with the mountains in the background, helping him write the assignment. It felt both perfectly natural and at the same time so unreal. We are usually well received in these villages, probably because we are such an oddity. We did, though, arrive in one where we were told to leave and some young boys threw stones at us. I believe they were protecting the privacy of the women.

And now again back in Lahore, I must tell you of a bit of excitement that took place the other morning. I was faced with 50-armed police when I arrived at the golf course. My caddy came over and told me that President Zia was arriving in about five minutes to play golf. To my surprise, I was not asked to leave, so hung around. One does not often get the chance to see the President, especially in such an informal situation. Many of the caddies were told they could not go to the first tee, but my friend Isobel & I were allowed to watch. It seemed so strange to see Zia in ordinary sports attire. His first shots were BAD and I felt sorry for him because a gallery of golf dignitaries accompanied him. He finally went on to the next tee followed by the crowd, and a waiter in full dress including a large gold hat, carrying a silver tray with a pot of coffee. A scene right out of the Raj.

Having mentioned snow on the mountains is as good a time as any to insert this snippet.

It would happen HERE when it snows! [handwritten annotation]

...ay, February 24, 1986.

Calamity hits areas of Rasool Nagar

BY A STAFF REPORTER

Areas of Rasool Nagar were hit by a natural calamity on Thursday evening. Mostly people thought the calamity was a wrath of God.

Heavy hailstorm hit the area and within minutes the land was covered with thick white snow. People ran helter-skelter and bowed their heads before Almighty Allah to beg forgiveness of their sins.

Social and religious workers appealed to the people to sink their differences and lead their lives according to the Quranic code of ethics. Sughra Kokhar, Second Headmistress of Government School, Rasool Nagar, appealed to the organisers of associations and 'anjumans' of various groups to spend their funds for the development of graveyards and for the sanitation of the area.

NOVEMBER, 1986

I have moved us out of our large bedroom into a smaller one and taken over the larger one for my studio. I need the small attached outdoor balcony to dry my thick paper pieces. I am attempting to get on with my paper work. It isn't easy. I am also working in the office and always have someone asking "Memsahib, is this to be done?" On the other hand, it sure is nice to have someone come in and clean up. I am just getting started because it has been too hot, so have no idea where it will take me. I wrote an article which is being published in Ontario Crafts Magazine, about setting up a papermaking studio in Pakistan. When I returned to Lahore, I looked for my 12-foot banana tree and discovered Mrs. Masood had thrown it out because in the monsoons, which took place while we were away, the tree had caused great problems with drainage. They were stored in the servant quarters and apparently, they blocked the drains. So, I am without banana pulp at the moment. I do have some sugar cane stalks and asked Qamar to help me cut up some of them on a small very old cutter that he had found for me. He cut the end off his finger and ended up in the emergency room, so I have decided not to recruit any more help. He cut off only a small tip and is reassured it will regrow, but still, I feel very responsible.

Last week I spent a great day in a small village with an American representative from the World Bank. She was investigating the idea of starting a small papermaking venture for the women. These women were all in purdah (wearing burqas) and have never been outside of the village. What a fascinating experience, but as soon they heard they would have to cook the pulp, they lost interest. Their small stoves are made of mud and fuelled by cow dung and hours of cooking sugar cane would not appeal to me either. We agreed this was not a practical idea. The women were lively and definitely knew what they did not want.

We just discovered today that we now have to have a visa to enter and re-enter Pakistan. We are heading to Nepal for Christmas, so today I went with Qamar (Dave is down with a flu bug) to the Visa office. It took over two hours and I forged Dave's name 10 times.

First we had to fill out four forms and then go over to a bank and deposit Rs35. We hopped into the car and headed for the bank. There, I received two sets of triplicate forms with no carbons, of course. I signed both our names (off in a corner) and returned to the original office, which consisted of two large desks, one light bulb hanging from the ceiling and thousands of forms sitting on the damp cement floor and piled right up to the ceiling. The six forms were eventually stamped, but then the official noted that we did not merely want an entry form; we were planning on leaving and re-entering. This was another ball game. "You will have to go back to the bank and pay another Rs-35 rupees. No I cannot accept the money here in this office." So we returned to the bank, filled out six more forms and came back. I again stood in a very long line and finally handed over the six forms and the receipt for the Rs-35 rupees. He very casually said that I would have to again fill out the same first four forms. I told him if this went on much longer we wouldn't need the visa because we were leaving the end of May. This is all for a single re-entry and we will have to repeat it all when we leave. I am surprised at the patience I have acquired.

Dave is still miserable with the flu and is on the phone trying to discuss something with someone at the Ministry. The conversation would make a good Bob Newhart recording and nudges Dave into thinking Canada may not seem so bad.

LATER IN NOVEMBER, 1986

I want to tell you about a fun time coming up (I hope). I have organized a golf tournament for a new group of Canadians who have arrived in the past six months. They are all with Ontario

Hydro and are a fun bunch. For most of our stay, we have been the only Canadians so we welcomed them with open arms. They are all younger and with young kids. Most of us are just taking up golf and got together a couple of weeks ago for a game. We tore up the turf so badly that I glibly christened us the Gophers. This gave me the idea of having a fun tournament. Life is always so serious here. Well, the tourney is now over and was great entertainment. We all wore bells attached to our hats to remind us to keep our heads down. I bought all sorts of crazy prizes including the one for the best far-fetched story on the course and the most "Oh Shit Shots." For the latter I gift-wrapped a huge cow dung (dried of course). At our house afterwards we were entertained by one of the Canadians on the guitar and of course we belted out all sorts of Christmas Carols. One of the Canadians had met a Peer (Prince) while on a project in Northern Pakistan and had invited him along. He was very suave and genteel and made us look like an undisciplined bunch of idiots. He won the "Most Times in the Sand Trap Award," which was a broom of the type used by the outdoor sweepers. The Peer has servants bowing as he passes and has probably never held a broom in his life. Getting into the spirit of things, he said he would put it in a vase and give it a place of honour and I think he will.

DECEMBER, 1986

It is now December, and we are leaving December 18 for Nepal and Delhi. We are told in our local paper that the troops along the Indian border are just on routine practice assignments, so hopefully there should be no problem.

The project is progressing slowly. The two million dollars worth of equipment that Dave ordered is supposed to be here around the middle of January and then things will get busy. Dave will be supervising the installation of this equipment into five Polytechnics in and around Lahore, and this entails that he travel to the various locations. I would like to travel with him, but unfortunately travelling with a woman here makes the situation so difficult for everyone involved. On one of our trips into a remote area, Dave and Qamar and I went into a restaurant for a cold drink. Before I knew what was happening to me, I was ushered by myself into a small stall and a curtain was pulled across. I lasted in there about five seconds.

On the home scene things are quite normal. Of course, that does not necessarily mean they are good. I hired our cook Martin because he was the exact opposite of arrogant, bossy, scheming, pouting Joseph. He is none of these things. In fact I am coming to the conclusion he is "not here." I have to program him every morning and if I need to change anything, deprogramming is almost impossible. He is pleasant and teaches me patience. Yesterday, he did not come to work, and his brother came over on the bike to tell us Martin was sick. A couple of days later Martin reappeared and I mentioned to him that I thought he was being sick a bit too often lately. He said, "I wasn't sick, Memsahib." I said "Your brother clearly told me you were sick, Martin." He said, "Maybe brother tell you that, but I was no sick, I was not well." I haven't tried to figure that one out yet.

It also didn't take me long to realize that desserts are not Martin's forte and his claim that he could read recipes was a bit exaggerated. Knowing this I bought some mango ice cream for one of his first dinner parties. I mashed up some fresh mangoes and mixed them with a bit of brandy to go over the ice cream. I felt he could probably handle cookies, so suggested he make some to go with the dessert. I also asked him to whip the ice cream and serve it in a large bowl. He brought the bowl of ice cream for me to serve and I waited for the topping and cookies. I finally decided to start serving the ice cream by itself and discovered he had mashed all the newly baked cookies and mixed them and the fruit in with the ice cream. It turned out to be delicious and we named it "ice cream a la Martin".

My favourite person continues to be Choti (little) Alice, our sweeper. She originally was only allowed to sweep outside. Joseph was upset when I said I was going to bring her inside as an indoor sweeper. He thought she was far beneath his status and his attitude showed in his daily disdain for her. Alice finally grew to the occasion when I decided to show her how to use an old vacuum that we had bought second hand. It was used only for the newly installed carpet in the living room. When I plugged in the vacuum, she jumped two feet, but once she got over the fear, it was fun to watch her. She grew in stature as she proudly whisked that vacuum around in front of Joseph. I bought her two cotton shalwar kameez and told her to shower each day before putting them on. We have a shower in the servant's quarters and she doesn't have running water in the adobe hut that she built with her own two hands.

She is my only female help and tells me when I am improperly dressed. This means too much arm or ankle showing. She supports six children, a blind mother, a drug-addicted husband, and she comes in every morning with a big smile. Her two sons, aged 11 and 12, are the only other two members earning money. One of them is a cripple and earns his money by sewing. The two sons each earn about the equivalent of $10 to $15 a month. I have grown to admire and love Alice and it will be difficult to leave her next May.

Last week she invited us to a party at her house for her son's birthday. I soon found out this was not a simple party. From somewhere, she borrowed enough money to buy rice, mutton and chappatis for the many relatives she had invited. It is considered their duty to come, many from far away villages to celebrate and give donations of money as their birthday gift. Hopefully, this money will cover the cost of the party with some left over. The many relatives arrived and were served food while they sat on charpoys in the dirt compound. Alice had borrowed two straight back wooden chairs for Dave and me, and there we sat in the middle of the compound smiling and drinking warm 7-up. Meanwhile, the husband, who to my surprise was both literate and sober, sat and recorded in a ledger the exact amount of each gift. The donor would expect Alice and her

husband to reciprocate at their next event. She informed me the next day with a triumphant smile that she did very well. Here are two photos of the event.

The birthday boy is the one with the hat. Please note the charpoys.

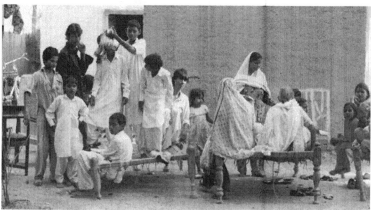

1987 LETTERS

January 10, 1987
50-G Gulberg 111
LAHORE, PAKISTAN
Phone 872711 (when it works)

I am sure you must think we have been caught in a cross fire or interned in a mosque. Such is not the case. I simply have not gotten around to writing since we got back from Nepal. At first it was too hot and now very busy. We wish you all a very happy 1987 and look forward to seeing you this summer. Our stay has been extended until the end of May.

Today I had an interview with the one and only public art gallery in Lahore, the National Art Gallery. If they accept, I will have an exhibition sometime this Spring. I have never been so totally unprepared, or so unworried about it. I will probably have a nervous breakdown about one week before. I have been told by the staff at the Art College that "You must show your work in the gallery because no one here has seen handmade paper as an art form." It came across as "It is your duty." When I expressed my doubts about having enough work in that time, Scherazade said "DON'T WORRY, Agnes, I will help you hang it and we can bring lots of plants from my house and my parents' house." So, here I am, committed.

APRIL 6, 1987

Hi Everyone,
Sorry I haven't written to you sooner, but we have been busy finishing the project and getting ready for my exhibition.

We had a wonderful Christmas in Nepal. We got our visas for India and Nepal two days before they stopped issuing them. The border situation was rather volatile. If we had gone at a warmer time, we would have taken a trip into Tibet, but it was just too cold and we were told the snow made the trip impassable. We actually rented down jackets, mitts, etc., in Nepal. Everyone should trek there for a few days at some time in his or her life. The mountain scenery is the most wondrous we have seen to date. We loved getting up a 5 a.m. to watch the sunrise. Every colour in the spectrum seemed to reflect off the Himalayas. We met many interesting people of all ages and nationalities. One night we sat on the dirt floor in a hut and I held a runny nose, but cheerful baby, while the wife cooked our meal over a small open fire. I could not believe my eyes when I was served spaghetti with a vegeterian sauce. It was delicious and we managed to live through it. The hygienic conditions in Nepal are pretty grim, but the country is beautiful once you get out of Katmandu, which has so much soul in spite of its filthiness.

We spent an entire day in a small pottery town. We could not move in the streets without almost tripping over pots or dogs. The potters' wheels are converted car tire rims and the boys learn the trade from an early age. One old man let me throw a pot on his wheel and was so amused watching me. I managed a small one, not an easy task on a tire rim.

We also visited a village about a 10-hour bus ride from Katmandu, where they make paper in the same way they did over 100 years ago. We stayed in a hostel at our lowest price yet,

25 cents a night. The owner of the small paper making shop took us to his house for tea and explained that the forests are being depleted and the materials for the paper (a type of tree bark) are now protected by the government. He is not sure if his business will be able to continue. It was a treat for me to sit and chat with another papermaker and to share our expertise and ideas with each other. He was fascinated with the idea that I was using bagasse.

It is now final that we leave for home on May 28th and arrive in Canada mid –July. We plan to fly out of Karachi to Istanbul, spend about ten days in Turkey, then a few days in Paris and eventually head for Lisbon. Our good friends here, Lars and Isobel, have offered us their house in Sintra, Portugal for a month and we are gratefully taking them up on the offer. Part of the month will be spent taking a rented car to Morocco with a short trip through Spain. We have a friend here who lives in Morocco and she will be there to show us around.

Dave is frantically busy now. Seventeen truckloads of equipment have arrived five months late. They have to be installed and the Instructors trained to use them. He is now trying to do all this in one month and the temperature is in the 100s F. Realizing how little time he has, two weeks before the equipment arrived, he started to make an Instructional Video on using the Trainers. These are electronic boards designed to teach students circuitry etc. and were specially designed for this project. This morning I found him with his head in the oven and his hand on the gas gauge. When he opened the equipment yesterday, they had sent different Trainers and a 3000-page booklet on how to use these new Trainers. I was tempted to join him in the oven, but we instead made coffee and said "Koi Battnay." No one worries about anything here, so why should we? Dave has enjoyed the freedom of action of the job and now I think the College back in Canada is going to seem rather stifling.

APRIL 19, 1987

WELL, DEAR FAMILY AND FRIENDS, I DID IT! My show is now hanging and I feel great. I wrote a long letter to Jo, my partner at the Forge, all about setting up the show, etc. Rather than rewrite the whole episode, I will copy it for you along with just a few of the many remarks written in my remarks book left at the gallery. I treasure them.

DEAR JO,
Nothing is done here until the last minute, but miraculously manages to get done (sometimes not too well). Six weeks before my show, I went to a printer named Asad, and said that I wanted a colour separation done and needed someone with studio lights to photograph my work for the invitation. I was told I could hire the photographer if I used the agency to design and print the invitation. I had intended to design my own card and write my own copy, but decided to accept their offer. They thought I was insane for starting so early, but I insisted and had them photograph my work.

A week later I called to see how things were developing and was told that the film they had used was special, could not be developed in Pakistan, and had been sent to London, England for processing - not to worry - it would only take ten days. At the end of ten days, I again called, and was informed that the film had been held up in Karachi and had never been sent to London. I was leaving for Islamabad at five the next morning and this was the day I was supposed to see the final layout. I had already done all the script, but we needed the photo. Asad very calmly informed me that he would have the film forwarded to London. I told him as calmly as I could "do not budge out of your studio, I will be right there." I arrived with a piece of my work and asked to have it photographed with a film that could be processed in Pakistan. I then, with great trepidation, left in the morning for Islamabad.

When I returned four days later, the photo was finished, but the piece had been photographed hanging very crooked on the wall. These are "professional photographers." Also, they had sent my script out to be redone, and it came back in a terrible format and full of errors. They said they could not correct them. There were apparently only two people working on computers in Lahore that were good enough for this type of reproduction, and it would take a few days. I had been calm up until this point, but now blew my cool and told them what I thought of their ineptness. This was not wise. I had injured the ego of two sensitive male artists. I had no choice but to leave everything in their hands and again call upon the help of Allah.

When I called a few days later to see if they were ready, I was told by Asad, in a very upset voice, that they resented being checked up on so often and it was obvious that I didn't trust them. I said "of course I trust you, it is your system I do not trust and I would like to see the final proof before it goes to print." Feathers were ruffled and I was told I would have to pay $50.US if I wanted to see the proof. I had hired him, he would do the job to perfection. "Koi Battnay" - the famous "don't worry." The alternative was that they wouldn't do it, and I could start over. It was now ten days before the show, so I had no choice. The next statement really put me in a flap. The invitations would definitely be ready in three more days IF THEY COULD GET THE PAPER on which to print them. I had already been informed they could not use my handmade paper. Once again Allah came through. The College of Art generously came up with enough paper for 500 invitations (the minimum number) Well, the invitations finally arrived five days before my opening. My first reaction was that they had a nice soft appearance, and the paper was great. Then I noticed that my piece was upside down on 500 invitations. On closer scrutiny I discovered four spelling mistakes and noted that three silver bands were blocking out a whole text that was not to be there. Two years ago, I would have wanted to put my hands around Asad's neck and squeeze until his eyes bulged, but having finally learned the true meaning of tolerance, I said as calmly and evenly as I could "My work is upside down, there are several errors, but I realize you have done your best, thank you," and left. I was so relieved to have anything to give out even though very late. I dropped some off at the Gallery and told Ahmeen the Curator, that the photo was upside down. He said "Don't worry, Agnes, no one will notice." I arrived home and handed an invitation to Choti Alice. She immediately turned the card upside down so the piece was correct. I should have hired Alice.

I must tell you how I did my pricing. I had no idea how to price the work, so one evening I had six artists from the Art College over for dinner. I gave them each a forbidden drink and a pencil and asked them to go around the house and price my work. I then took an average. It was difficult for them because they had never seen handmade paper in this form. I sold 15 of the 54 pieces and was told I would probably have had a sell out if I had priced them lower. I felt a responsibility to Pakistan Artists, and didn't want to put low prices just for the sake of selling. I am quite happy to take them back to Canada.

Next came the hanging and this was when I was really thinking of you Jo, because we have hung so many shows together so easily, and I thought of us sitting on the floor of the Forge Gallery with a bottle of wine, leisurely deciding which pieces should go where.

The Alhamra Gallery is part of a very recently opened Art Complex and very elaborate and modern for Lahore. It consists of three large Galleries and a large theatre complex. I felt quite intimidated by the huge two stories high gallery with a large spiral staircase joining the two spaces. I was concerned about not having enough work to fill the entire space. Sheherazade who had offered to help me hang and also fill the spaces with plants, informed me that there was to be a wedding in the family in Islamabad and she had to go, or the family would be devastated. I understood, because weddings are command performances for family, but to say I was devastated is an understatement. My good friend Isobel came to the rescue and helped me hang. I had, at my own expense, had six 8 foot panels made to try and break some of the high wall space. I had them sewn by a local stitcher who sits out on the sidewalk in the bazaar. Of course he overcharged, and when I attempted to hang the first one, I discovered that he had not left the hem large enough for the rods. Good old Qamar came again to my rescue. He got his wife's sewing machine, sat on the floor in the middle of the gallery, and restitched all the panels.

The ceilings are eleven or twelve feet high, and you must get on this gigantic ladder to hang each piece. We were offered the assistance of three boys who spoke no English, but who had to keep running up and down the ladder while Isobel and I swung our arms pointing in which direction to move the pieces. The other two didn't know what to do, but kept busy holding the ladder. I had been promised ten boxes to display some sitting pieces, and two days before the opening, six unpainted wooden boxes appeared. I asked three times if I could please have them painted white and kept getting the answer "yes." I suggested that perhaps the two extra helpers could let go of the ladder and paint the boxes. It came to light that this could not happen because it was a half day holiday, and there would not be time. The day before the opening they were painted, after I threatened to do it myself.

While attempting to hang the show, people kept coming into the gallery talking loudly and generally getting in the way. Finally I told Ahmeen, we could not concentrate with all these people and would he please ask them to leave and then lock the doors until the opening. It turned out I had kicked out three top members of the Lahore Arts Council and a leading reporter. The next day in her paper, I got two lines printed over a photograph of one of my pieces, again hanging upside down. I did get two very nice newspaper reviews that I will try and copy for you.

Both of the Pakistani writers seemed to understand and appreciate that I had chosen to use every day objects and materials from the markets and fields, so the viewers would realize that "Art" is found in simple forms. As you will see in the letters, one writer thought my work was "Witchcraft." With the exception of a few young contemporary artists, what I have seen shown in Lahore as Art, are traditional style paintings following in the steps of European Masters. My exhibition has clearly been a challenge in understanding for many, and thankfully inspirational for some.

And so to continue; miraculously, the show went on, and I had a large crowd in attendance. Alhamra is a public gallery and charges no commission on sales. I paid for all expenses with the exception of refreshments. I had asked members of the Canadian Embassy if they would give some financial assistance and if they would do me the honour of opening the exhibition. I never got a response. Dave's firm generously offered to help with the expenses. I thought it would be fun and appropriate to have the sugar cane stand in front of the gallery and serve sugar cane juice, since this is where I got the bagasse for my paper. Ahmeen, said "Oh no Agnes, that is not possible, because people only drink sugar cane in the morning." Now I know this is not the case, but was too tired to argue, so everyone was handed a warm bottle of soda.

Sheherazade flew back from Islamabad in time to give an opening address. She gave a very sensitive speech, and placed a big garland of flowers around my neck. Later in the evening I had a big party back at our apartment, and my generous Canadian friends brought finger foods. The fact that so many friends were helping gave me the wonderful feeling of community and I again realized looking from abroad, what a great group the Canadians are.

As we were locking up the doors to leave the gallery, I told Ahmeen that I would drop in and visit him the next day. That was when I discovered that Ahmeen would not be in the Gallery. He was leaving town and it was my responsibility to man the Gallery for the entire month. And yet another surprise.

We leave to go home to Canada in a few weeks after a very fulfilling three years. I was asked to keep the show on longer because it is getting such a large response, but unfortunately it is too close to our leaving and packing. As a result of the exhibition, I also gave two more workshops to Art Teachers in Lahore. I left a Remarks Book at the Gallery and some of the comments are priceless. I will copy some for you. Many are in Urdu, but Sheherazade has translated them for me.

See you back at the Forge.
Agnes

Dear Aunty!
I am really surprised that
You made a fool of every one
by this exibition from the
gorbage bin but all the same
your idea is very unique to
utilize gorbage in this
manner. I think this is
a new form of witch
Craft.

Shamsa Zia
F. J. M. C

I really want to see
you !!!

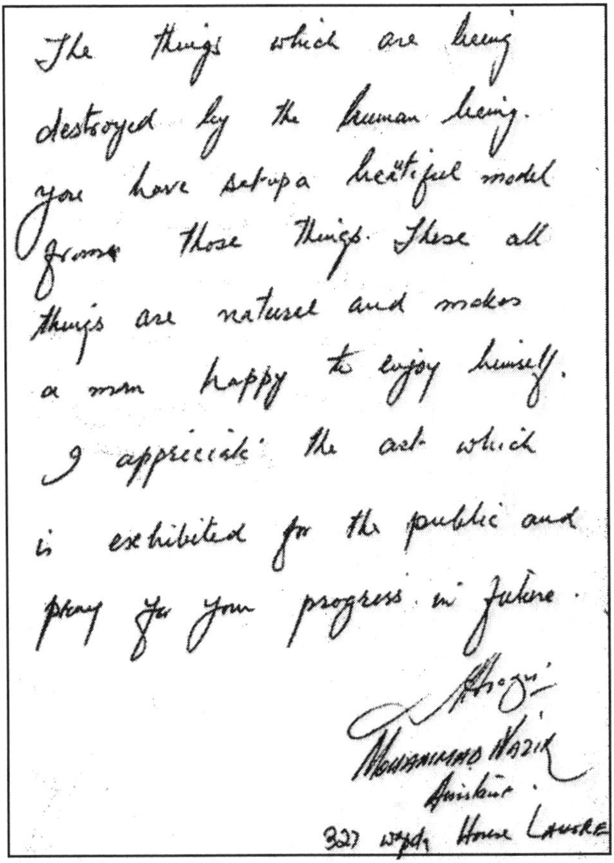

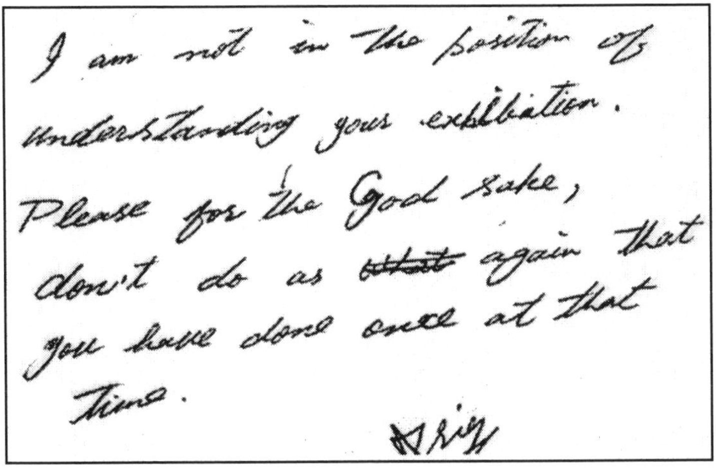

Agnes,
You helped in opening many many doors last year at N.C.A. This is the highpoint of that experience. Thank you My students join me in expressing their congratulations & appreciation

Naazish Ata-Ullah

I put pressure on my mind to understand it, But it is above to my understanding.

TAHIR HAMID

The job what' Mrs AgnesOlive has done for the representation of Pakistan's Enroirment ——— is extremly excellent.

The symbolic Touchs are very meaningful and this handmade products are a beautiful chepter for those who say that after the inventions the man is) living a far away from nature.

The quite people can't live away from Natur's friendship

12/4/1987   TARIQ MAHMOOD

Editor: THE RAVIANS Digest.
THE STAR HOUSE, G-687, LAHORE-8,
LAHORE, PAKISTAN

My show closes tomorrow and today there was a bomb scare at the Alhamra Gallery. I felt quite important that my exhibition had caused such a stir but was informed that it was quite unlikely the case. They still don't know the reason for the threat. I was accused of Witchcraft by a couple of viewers, but think bombing would be a bit drastic.

MAY, 1987

Dave and I are leaving Pakistan with reluctance. In some aspects it has been an easy way of life and we have made such good friends. It will be great to see family and friends in Canada and we are also going home to the excitement of holding our first grandchild. Steve and Natalie are expecting in August and we will be there for the big event. Everyone is very happy with the results of the project and have complimented Dave on a job well done. He has completed a new curriculum of studies, overseen the purchase of new electronic laboratory equipment and trained the teachers how to use it. During the last few months he has been under much time pressure and now will have a well deserved restful and exciting trip home.

I could not end this letter without a final story on our domestic scene. It is as strange as ever. Qamar is in jail. He is accused of Aiding and Abetting. We still don't have the whole story and probably never will, but it involves another woman, an irate and sobbing wife, an irate and vindictive husband, an irate and greedy mother of the other woman who is threatening to get together a mob and storm Qamar's house, and the usual police payola, etc. In other words, all the makings of a Pakistani movie. What I have heard from the other servants is that Qamar introduced a Muslim woman to a Christian man. I have cause to believe they held their trysts at our apartment while we were away. As if this weren't enough, they are both married. We are concerned for Qamar's safety because we have heard of many horror tales about being in jail. Also, this comes at a very crucial time for us because we desperately need his help.

We went for advice to our Guru, Mrs. Masood, who told us we must never go near the jail or his bail will be tripled. We are to stay out of it and she would see what was going on and if we can help behind the scenes. And so we wait. His wife has been at our house crying and we feel sorry for her and at the same time want to kill Qamar for being so stupid. People take "illicit relations" very seriously as you have seen by the paper snippets. Qamar may find that he is safer in jail. Of course since he has been my guide and cohort for three years, I miss having him around and as I said, we are concerned for his safety.

That was the very last letter that I sent because we had to pack up our computer and all the stuff we were taking back. That is another story. A few days before we were to leave, we discovered that we had figured out our shipping allowance incorrectly and could only take approximately half of what we had packed. I still remember vividly sitting in the middle of a field surrounded by boxes. They had to be unpacked and many things left behind. Dave was busy at the office, so I had to make the decisions of what to take or leave behind. It was a nightmare. The temperature was in the 100s F and a group of friends were waiting at the American Club to give us a farewell party. The people at shipping were waiting for our boxes to arrive. I gave away many things and then the wonderful Canadians again came to our rescue and said they would slip in a box or two if they had room in their shipments. Through the next year we gradually received a box here and there, and we are forever grateful to our dear friends.

Qamar was still in Jail when we left, but he was eventually released and we are told that he bounced right back on his feet as a driver for an American family. Martin was hired as cook at the American Club and serves his famous pudding. Alice became a nanny for friends of ours, and the last we heard, both she and our friends are happy. I often ponder what takes place in our souls when we touch other lives. I am not the same person I was in 1984. I am enriched by my many experiences and hope those I have touched are also more enlightened about our culture and our "Ways of Seeing."

A happy Agnes at the opening

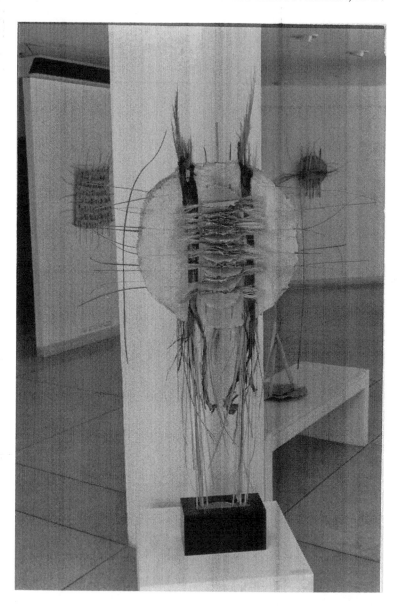

Paper exhibition

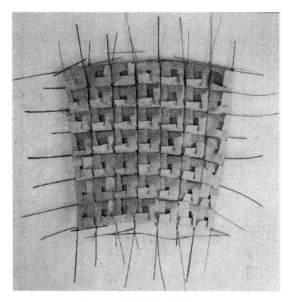

ways of seeing

There are many ways of seeing, but the truest, and best is with the intuition, for it takes in the whole, whereas the intellect only takes in a part.

Soetsu Yanagi
"The Unknown Craftsman"

ABOUT THE EXHIBITION

This Exhibition is about Materials, Explorations, Observations, Communication. It is an introduction to the public of Hand Made Paper as a two and three Dimensional Art Form. For the past two years, Agnes Olive, A Canadian Artist living in Lahore, has gathered meterials from the local markets, street vendors and the countryside in an attempt to use only readily available indigenous materials for ther Hand Made Paper.

The Rural Countryside with its abundance of Grasses and small Mud Dwellings has been the inspiration for many of the forms presented in this Exhibition. The artist has enjoyed exploring both this medium and the country of Pakistan and now wishes to share with the public her emotional responses, her perceptions, her "Way of Seeing"

Using paper as an art form

From Javed Bashir

How the inexorable advance of mechanisation consigned many indigenous arts and crafts to oblivion is a phenomenon that almost all countries have experienced. But the worst sufferers in the process were the developing countries where quite a few local art forms suffered neglect and fell into desuetude.

In Pakistan, for example, the age-old method of using paper as an art form was once practised in some areas. Now, ironically, the craft has been resurrected by someone unaware of its existence in these parts — a foreigner, Agnes Olive, a Canadian artist living in Lahore. An exhibition featuring 50 artistic designs she made from material found in the country was inaugurated on Sunday at the Alhamra Art Centre.

The rural milieu influenced her greatly during her extensive travels through Pakistan and provided the subjects reflected in her art. "I love your villages. My inspiration comes from there, because everything there is so very natural," she said.

Agnes, before coming to Pakistan three years ago, had not the slightst inkling that the bazars and streets of Pakistan, particularly the rural expanse, would present such rich raw material which would lend itself to aesthetic moulds. Probably this is because, she says, that "I see your country from a different eye", to be able to utilise local material for artistic fulfilment.

For Agnes, whose works are based on bagasse, reeds from brooms, palm stalks, coconut fibre, seeds and stems, this is an entirely "self-exploratory effort". Her training as an artist comes in handy in the shaping and designing of the materials collected from local street vendors. A graduate of the Sheridan College of Design, Toronto, she is a member of the American Association of Artists Therapists. In Canada she works as a professional artist specialising in Raku clay, a Japanese type of pottery. Agnes, who has a studio and an art gallery in Terra Cota, Ontario, has also set up a paper-making studio in her house in Lahore.

The influence of the Lahore environment is manifest in many of her works. Notable among them, for example, is a three-dimensional design featuring folded squares of bagasse pinioned to a frame made of stem. The katchi abadis' ambience inspired it. Her fascination for the charpoy led to another construction of handmade paper sheets interspersed with stalks of banana bark. Some of the baskets on display reveal a similar ingenuity to give artistic meaning to the raw material employed.

Due to the medium utilised perhaps, some of the designs give a sharp cubic effect. Agnes, however, denies any conscious effort to draw on the art movements that influenced many distinguished artits of her time. The artist, nevertheless, accepts the influence on the forms developed of the visual experiences gained during travels to different regions. "It is not possible that you travel and bring nothing", says Agnes, who has been to China, Kenya, Japan, Nepal and India.

The African visit showed up in some of the icons presented in the exhibition and the journeys through India also influenced her present art. The idea of using paper as an art form, however, came to her during her tour of Japan, where she visited many paper-making villages. Japanese culture seems to have impressed her immensely and its simplicity permeates throughout her innovative designs. While some local cultures figured prominently in the improvisations, the artist nonetheless brings to bear an international perspective on her art.

The exhibition provides an artistic experience to art lovers and students of indigenous crafts and enables them to appreciate better the possibilities offered by the material used by the artist.

Marcella Co Nesom

HANDMADE paper from local bagasse (sugar cane scraps) combined with banana tree bark, wild reeds from sweeper's brooms, tori (dried vegetable core), coconut fibres, plant stalks, seeds and stems are the essence and raw materials of Agnes Olive's constructions.

Her exquisitely crafted and imaginative creations should speak to the man-in-the-street as well as the sophisticated art conroisseur. Everyone can relate to the materials. They are ubiquitous, particularly bagasse at this time of year. Next time you take a glass of sugar cane juice from a roadside stand and notice the heap of bagasse lyhing along side, you might ponder on the transformation from scraps to Agnes's finely molded handmade paper. Agnes has become a scavenger, seeking out her raw materials, then stripping, pulling at them, soaking them and incorporating selected pieces into her multiformed constructions.

Some hang on the wall, some dangle from the rafters, some sit comfortably as baskets, others stand tall and graceful from handmade boxes. She eschews artificial colour, which in my opinion is a wise choice. There is a myriad of natural colour in plant life and Agnes is drawn to the dirfectnoss and subtlety of organic things. Her constructions vibrate with life communicating through texture (intrinsic to the material itself and created by Agnes in the process of combining fibres to the damp paper), through movement and the play of shadows.

Some of the pieces are a conscious reflection of the Lahore environment, others are a subconscious articulation of past visual experiences. A series of folded squares strung on a plant stem frame were inspired by the katchi abadis that impressed Agnes as fascinating textural structures with beautiful soft hues delineating the windows. Another series of flat square handmade paper sheets criss-crossed with banana bark stalks were certainly inspired by charpoy construction. So intrigued by the charpoy design, Agnes had one specially made (sans legs) to hang on her wall and then made one herself adding a few extra flourishes to hang on a nearby wall.

A group of baskets are consummate designs of simplicity and economy of materials. Agnes has cleverly joined the plant stalk handles by looping the plant stalk handles through the paper catching the stalks and piercing the tops of handles with a thin stem adding to the design quality and performing the n ecessary function of joining the handle together.

A group of three standing guarding icons are easily related to her recent African trip. Though delicate looking, these sculptural talismans (like all her other pieces) are strong and sturdy and remarkably flexible. Other round shield-like constructions seem to be likewise inspired by the African trip.

Alhamra exhibition on April 12

Paper exhibition

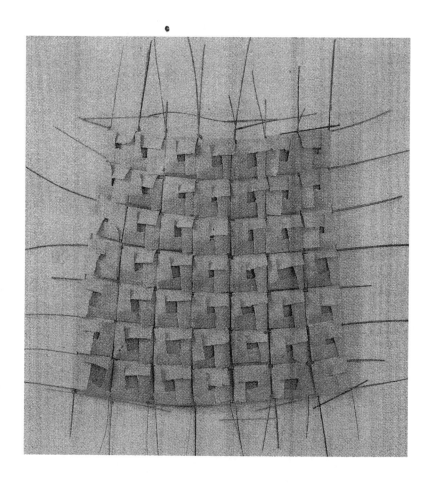

Paper exhibition

Paper exhibition

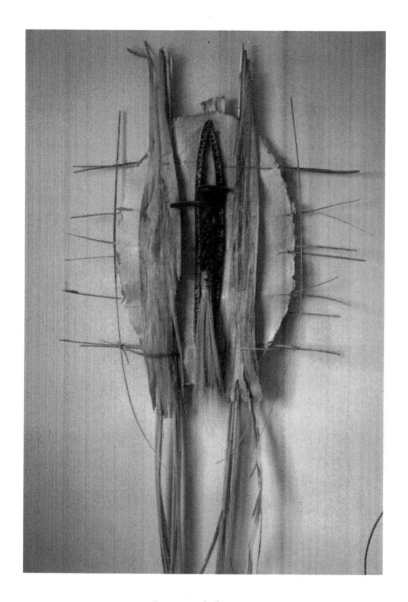

Paper exhibition